MW00992852

Gooseberry Patch

Celebrate Year 'Round

A Country Store In Your Mailbox®

Gooseberry Patch
600 London Road
P.O. Box 190
Delaware, OH 43015

★

1·800·854·6673

www.gooseberrypatch.com

Copyright 2005, Gooseberry Patch 1-931890-57-9
Third Printing, September, 2006

All rights reserved. No part of this book may be reproduced or utilized in any form
or by any means, electronic or mechanical, including photocopying and recording,
or by any information storage and retrieval system, without permission in writing
from the publisher.

Do you have a tried & true recipe...

tip, craft or memory that you'd like to see featured in a **Gooseberry
Patch** book? Visit our web site at **www.gooseberrypatch.com**,
register and follow the easy instructions to submit your favorite family
recipe. Or send them to us at:

Gooseberry Patch
Attn: Book Dept.
P.O. Box 190
Delaware, OH 43015

Don't forget to include the number of servings your recipe makes, plus
your name, street address, phone number and e-mail address! If we
select your recipe, your name will appear right along with it...and you'll
receive a FREE copy of the book!

Contents

Celebrate Autumn...................5

Indian Summer Picnic.......................... 6
Tailgate Gathering............................ 12
Frightful Fun on All-Hallow's Eve............... 20
Come for Soup................................ 26
Remembering Thanksgiving.................... 42

Celebrate Winter..................... 53

Cozy Winter Warmers........................54
Yuletide Candlelight Dinner....................62
Christmas Morning.......................... 72
Welcoming in the New Year....................78
Nothing but Chocolate........................88
Hearts Afire..................................98

Celebrate Spring..................... 105

Luck O' the Irish............................. 106
Spring Buffet................................ 116
Country Wedding............................. 130
Especially for Mom........................... 142
Garden Party................................ 152

Celebrate Summer.................. 163

All-American Cookout......................... 164
Dads & Grads............................... 174
Blue-Ribbon Winners......................... 184
Old-Fashioned Ice Cream Social............... 194
Tex-Mex Feast.............................. 206

Dedication

To everyone who finds delight in each changing season.

Appreciation

*Many thanks to all of our **Gooseberry Patch** friends, who inspire us every day of the year.*

Celebrate Autumn

Indian Summer Picnic

Fresh Veggie Pizza

This crunchy portable snack recipe can be adapted to your favorite vegetables. Try experimenting with additional ingredients like olives, mushrooms and green peppers.

2 tubes refrigerated
   crescent rolls
2 8-oz. pkgs. cream cheese,
   softened
1 c. mayonnaise
1 pkg. dry ranch salad
   dressing mix

1/4 c. green onion, sliced
1/2 c. carrots, shredded
1/4 c. cauliflower flowerets
1/4 c. broccoli flowerets
1/2 c. tomatoes, chopped
3/4 c. Cheddar cheese,
   shredded

Press crescent roll dough onto pizza pan. Bake at 350 degrees for 10 minutes. Mix cream cheese, mayonnaise and dressing mix; spread on baked crust. Top with vegetables; press into cream cheese mixture. Sprinkle with Cheddar cheese. Refrigerate, covered, for 2 hours. Serves 8.

The best of all sauces is exercise in the open air and, equally, the best of digestives is pleasant company.
–St. Ange

Spicy Black Bean Salsa

A quick and easy low-fat salsa, hot as you like!

8-oz. can black beans,
    drained and rinsed
2/3 c. corn relish
1/4 c. onion, minced

2 t. lime juice
1/4 t. cumin
hot pepper sauce to taste

Stir all ingredients together and allow to stand, covered, for 30 minutes. Serve with baked pita chips. Makes about 2 cups.

Crunchy Baked Pita Chips

Chewier and fresher-tasting than bagged chips.

4 large rounds pita bread
1 t. garlic powder

Split pita bread rounds, then cut into wedges. Sprinkle with garlic powder and bake in a single layer at 350 degrees for 10 to 12 minutes, or until crisp. Store in airtight container. Makes 4 dozen.

You may find a listing of bike paths in your area at the local library. There are few better ways to enjoy the fall colors than a tree-lined bike path, under canopies of red, russet and gold.

Picnic Barbecued Chicken Sandwiches

These are delicious hot or cold, depending on where you'll be enjoying them.

3 lbs. boneless, skinless chicken, cooked and shredded
1 c. catsup
1-3/4 c. water
1 onion, finely chopped
1 t. salt

1 t. celery seed
1 t. chili powder
1/4 c. brown sugar, packed
1 t. hot pepper sauce
1/4 c. Worcestershire sauce
1/4 c. red wine vinegar
6 Kaiser rolls

Combine all ingredients except rolls in large saucepan and simmer for 1-1/2 hours. Pile onto Kaiser rolls. Serves 6.

Keep chicken sandwiches and other cold foods cold by packing a few frozen juice boxes in with your picnic treats.

Favorite Peanut Butter Cookies

For extra crunch, add whole peanuts to the batter.

1/2 c. butter, softened
1/2 c. sugar
1/2 c. brown sugar,
   packed
1 large egg

1 c. creamy or crunchy
   peanut butter
1/2 t. baking soda
1/2 t. vanilla extract
1-1/4 c. all-purpose flour

Preheat oven to 350 degrees. Cream butter and sugars until light and fluffy. Add egg, peanut butter, baking soda and vanilla and beat until smooth. Add flour in portions, beating until well mixed. Shape balls out of teaspoonfuls of the dough and arrange on greased baking sheets. Flatten balls with tines of a fork, making a pattern. Bake in center of oven about 12 minutes, or until golden. Makes 5-1/2 dozen cookies.

Spiced Apple Cider

*Is there anything that tastes
more like autumn than cider?*

3 qts. apple cider
12 whole cloves
10 whole allspice
1 T. candied ginger
10 cinnamon sticks
3/4 c. brown sugar,
   packed

Combine all ingredients except sugar and boil. Lower heat, add sugar and simmer 15 to 20 minutes. Strain and pack in a thermos container to serve steaming hot. Makes 3 quarts.

Great ideas...

Applesauce Leather

Kids love this delicious, portable snack with just 3 ingredients. Just take a 16-ounce jar of applesauce and season with 1/4 teaspoon cinnamon and 1/2 teaspoon lemon juice. Purée the mixture until smooth. Spread it on a large piece of plastic wrap so that it measures about 1/4-inch thick. Let it dry in the oven, with the door slightly ajar, at 150 degrees about 6 to 8 hours, or until it feels somewhat dry but still tacky. Remove it from the plastic wrap, rolling it into a jelly-roll shape. Then cut it into smaller portions. Store, covered, in your refrigerator or in a cooler.

Framed Leaves

Everyone agrees, autumn leaves are a work of art. Why not frame them? Make a simple mounting board with a piece of cork from a building supply store; just have the cork cut to fit inside a wooden frame. Old worn frames look best...they have that antique look we love. You can cover the cork with fabric to complement your colors. Just stretch the fabric over the cork and staple to the back. Arrange leaves and glue to the fabric. Then fit the cork inside the frame and use a tack hammer to pound tacks or fine nails through the cork and the back of the frame. Attach a fine wire or sawtoothed brad to the back for hanging.

Decorated Pots

There are so many ways to decorate terra cotta pots! Gather colorful leaves, pine cones, acorns, seed pods, dried berries and cattails and arrange into a pleasing pattern. Then hot glue your treasures to flowerpots. Use a large pot with a candle as a centerpiece, or fill smaller pots with potpourri.

Golden Wheat Bundles

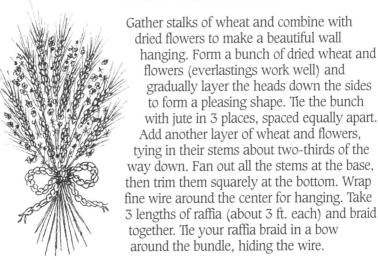

Gather stalks of wheat and combine with dried flowers to make a beautiful wall hanging. Form a bunch of dried wheat and flowers (everlastings work well) and gradually layer the heads down the sides to form a pleasing shape. Tie the bunch with jute in 3 places, spaced equally apart. Add another layer of wheat and flowers, tying in their stems about two-thirds of the way down. Fan out all the stems at the base, then trim them squarely at the bottom. Wrap fine wire around the center for hanging. Take 3 lengths of raffia (about 3 ft. each) and braid together. Tie your raffia braid in a bow around the bundle, hiding the wire.

Tailgate Gathering

Soft Pretzels with Mustard

*You may want to triple this recipe...these warm, chewy
pretzels are very popular!*

2 pkgs. active dry yeast
1-1/2 c. warm water
4-1/2 c. all-purpose flour
1/2 t. salt

1/4 c. baking soda in
1 c. water
yellow, Dijon and spicy
brown mustards

Dissolve yeast in warm water. Sift flour into large bowl. Add
yeast and salt to flour. Mix well and allow to rise for about
15 minutes. Divide dough into 12 equal portions; roll into
8-inch ropes. Place in a shallow pan in baking soda solution; let
stand for 2 minutes. Form into desired shapes and place on a
greased baking sheet. Sprinkle with additional salt as desired.
Bake at 350 degrees for 20 minutes. Serve with an assortment
of mustards. Makes one dozen.

*No tickets to the big game? Have a tailgate party
anyway! Soak up the atmosphere by going to a local
high school pep rally or pre-game party. Wear the
team colors and cheer them on.*

Running Back Popcorn & Peanuts

You'll go "running back" for more!

1/2 c. honey
1/4 c. butter

6 c. popped popcorn
1 c. salted peanuts

Heat honey and butter until blended. Mix popcorn and peanuts in a large bowl, and stir in honey butter mixture. Spread mixture into 2 large pans. Bake for 10 minutes at 350 degrees. Makes 7 cups.

No one knows who discovered popcorn, but it's been around for centuries. In ancient times, it was believed that each popcorn kernel had a little devil inside. When the kernel was heated, the little devil became so angry that he burst through the hull trying to escape. The Aztecs used popcorn as decoration on headdresses, statues and in good luck ceremonies. It is believed that popcorn was introduced to the English colonists at the first Thanksgiving.

Championship Artichoke Dip

Try serving this hot, cheesy dip in a scooped-out round of sourdough bread. Just brush the insides with olive oil and bake in a 350-degree oven for 10 minutes.

2 c. Parmesan cheese, grated
2 c. mozzarella cheese, grated
1 c. mayonnaise
2 cloves garlic, finely chopped
16-oz. can artichoke hearts, drained and finely chopped
assorted crackers

Mix all ingredients thoroughly. Bake at 375 degrees for 45 minutes. Serve with assorted crackers. Makes 7 cups.

Halftime Tomato-Basil Soup

A thermos of this spicy soup will warm you to your toes.

1 large onion, chopped
1/2 c. butter
6 tomatoes, chopped
2/3 c. sherry or chicken broth
6 to 8 fresh basil leaves
1 c. Cheddar cheese, grated

Sauté onion in butter until golden. Add tomatoes, sherry and basil; partly cover and simmer 30 minutes. Mash large chunks of tomato with a potato masher. Top with cheese. Makes 4 to 6 servings.

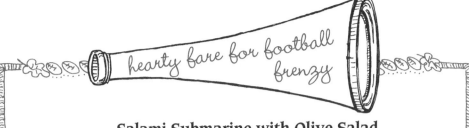

Salami Submarine with Olive Salad

A favorite craving of some men we know.

18-inch long loaf crusty
French bread
1/4 lb. Genoa salami,
thinly sliced

1/4 lb. Swiss cheese,
thinly sliced

Slice the bread lengthwise but do not cut all the way through to the other side. Scoop out some of the bread from each half. Divide the olive salad and pack into each half. Layer salami and cheese in rows down each half of the sandwich. Close the halves together and wrap tightly in heavy aluminum foil. To fully blend the flavors, place heavy books on top of the sandwich and allow it to rest for a couple of hours. When ready to serve, slice into 2-inch portions. Serves 9.

Olive Salad:

3 c. Greek, green and
black olives
7-oz. jar roasted red peppers,
drained and chopped
2 T. capers

1/2 c. fresh parsley, chopped
1/4 c. fresh basil, chopped
2 cloves garlic, crushed
3 T. red wine vinegar
6 T. olive oil

Toss all ingredients together and store in a tightly covered glass jar in the refrigerator. This salad improves with age and is delicious on many sandwiches.

Put your foil-wrapped sub in the oven for 20 minutes, then sprinkle Italian dressing under the bun for a hot, crisp treat. For extra tang, add banana peppers too.

Tailgate Gathering

Smothered Hot Dogs

The longer they simmer, the better they taste.

1/2 small onion, minced
1 can beer
1 T. Worcestershire sauce

1/4 c. chili sauce
12 all-beef hot dogs
12 hot dog buns

Mix onion, beer, Worcestershire sauce and chili sauce in a saucepan. Add hot dogs and simmer for 30 minutes, stirring occasionally. Serve dogs and sauce on buns. Serves 12.

Confetti Salad

You may use bottled dressing, or make your own with a little oil, tarragon or wine vinegar and a touch of sugar.

1 zucchini, shredded
1 carrot, shredded
1 green pepper, shredded
1 yellow squash, shredded

1 red pepper, shredded
1/3 c. vinaigrette or
    sweet-and-sour dressing

Shred all vegetables together and toss with dressing.
Serves 4 to 6.

Listen! the wind is rising,
and the air is wild
with leaves.
We have had our
summer evenings,
now for October eves!
-Humbert Wolfe

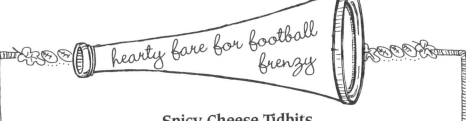

Spicy Cheese Tidbits

Use fun shapes of cookie cutters to cut out bread...autumn leaves, acorns or crescent moons.

8-oz. pkg. pasteurized
   processed cheese spread,
   cubed
1 c. butter, softened
1 t. onion, grated

hot pepper sauce to taste
1 egg, beaten
1 loaf whole-wheat bread,
   sliced

Blend together cheese and butter; add onion, sauce and egg. Cut shapes out of bread with cookie cutters. Spread mixture on bread; bake on a greased baking sheet for about 3 minutes at 450 degrees. Makes 2 to 3 dozen.

Buckeye Candy

We pay homage to an Ohio tradition.

1 lb. butter, softened
2 lbs. creamy peanut butter
3 lbs. powdered sugar

3 c. dipping chocolate,
   melted

Cream together butter and peanut butter. Add powdered sugar and blend well. Shape mixture by hand into buckeye-sized balls. Place on baking sheet and refrigerate for one hour. Melt dipping chocolate in top of double boiler. Using a toothpick, dip balls into chocolate three-quarters of the way up. Place on waxed paper and allow to cool. Makes about 200 buckeyes. Can be frozen for 2 to 3 weeks.

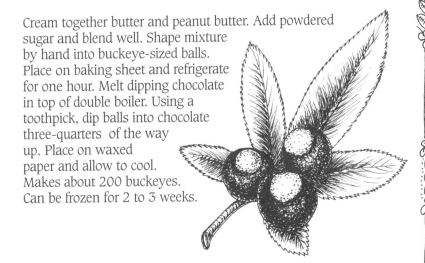

End Zone Brownies

So easy...add chocolate chips for even more rich flavor.

1/2 c. butter, softened
1 c. sugar
4 eggs, beaten
16-oz. can chocolate syrup
1 t. vanilla extract

1 c. plus 1 T. all-purpose
flour
1 c. chopped walnuts
Garnish: powdered sugar

Mix all ingredients together; pour into a large greased jelly-roll pan. Bake at 350 degrees for 20 to 22 minutes. Cool for 10 minutes. Remove from pan; dust with powdered sugar. Makes 3 dozen.

> *By all these lovely tokens*
> *September days are here,*
> *With summer's best of weather*
> *And autumn's best of cheer.*
> *-Helen Hunt Jackson*

Break out the fall cookie cutters...autumn leaves, acorns, squirrels. Trace around them to make stencils, then place stencils on your brownies and dust with powdered sugar for fun fall designs.

Fun & fancy...

Soda Pop Buckets

If you're having a party for the Big Game (or any occasion where friends gather), it's fun to serve bottles or cans of soft drinks in big buckets filled with ice. Inexpensive metal buckets are easy to decorate with your team colors. Just rub the bucket with steel wool and paint it overall with a base color, using 2 coats of enamel paint. After the base color dries, paint the design of your choice onto the bucket with different enamels. Let dry for 6 hours between contrasting coats of paint. The buckets can be given away as prizes...or save them for the next party!

Colorful Apple Baskets

Those pretty red-handled wooden apple baskets are beautiful filled with bundles of sunny fall grasses and flowers. Try any combination of strawflowers, everlastings, roses, pussy willow, cattails, yarrow and hydrangeas. Paint your basket freehand, or use stencils to brush on a pretty design. (You can use cookie cutters to make stencils.)

Frightful Fun on All-Hallow's Eve

Goblin Cheese Balls

Kids and adults alike love this melty cheese appetizer.

1 c. Cheddar cheese,
  shredded
3 T. butter, softened
1/2 c. all-purpose flour

dash of paprika
dash of salt
3.8-oz. jar pimento-stuffed
  green olives, drained

In a small bowl, blend all ingredients except olives to make a dough. Mold one teaspoon dough around each green olive, covering completely. Arrange in an ungreased pan and bake at 400 degrees for 12 minutes. Makes 16 appetizers.

Midnight Moon Sandwiches

Of course you can vary the sandwich fillings. Try this recipe with chicken or turkey.

1 tube refrigerated crescent
  rolls
1/2 lb. cooked ham, thinly
  sliced

1 c. Monterey Jack cheese,
  shredded
1 egg, beaten
2 T. butter, melted

Open crescent rolls and place on large baking sheet. Layer ham and cheese in the middle of each crescent. Roll into crescents and pinch together edges to seal. Brush tops with egg and melted butter. Bake in 350-degree oven for 15 minutes, or until golden brown. Allow to cool before serving. Makes 8 sandwiches.

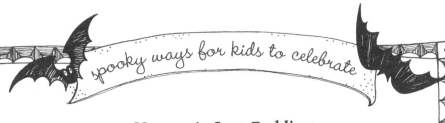

Mummy's Corn Pudding

If you have it, try this dish using fresh sweet corn. Yum!

16-oz. can corn, drained
16-oz. can creamed corn
2 eggs, beaten
8-oz. pkg. corn muffin mix

1/2 c. butter, melted
1 c. sour cream
2 c. Cheddar cheese,
  shredded

Mix all ingredients together except cheese. Pour into a greased 13"x9" baking dish. Bake at 350 degrees for 15 minutes. Sprinkle with cheese; bake 15 minutes longer. Makes 6 servings.

Frightfully Good Apple-Cheddar Bread

Apples and Cheddar cheese go together…it's as simple as that!

3 c. all-purpose flour
1/2 c. sugar
2 T. baking powder
3/4 t. salt
1 egg, beaten
1 egg yolk, beaten

1-1/2 c. milk
1/2 c. vegetable oil
3/4 c. apples, cored, peeled
  and diced
3/4 c. Cheddar cheese,
  shredded

Combine flour, sugar, baking powder and salt in a large mixing bowl. Combine whole egg, egg yolk, milk and oil in a medium bowl; add to flour mixture and stir just until moistened. Gently fold in apples and cheese. Divide batter among 3 greased 8"x4" loaf pans. Bake at 350 degrees for about 40 minutes, until a toothpick comes out clean. Cool 10 minutes and remove from pans. When completely cool, wrap in plastic wrap and store in the refrigerator. Makes 3 loaves.

Mini pumpkins and gourds look festive in a fall centerpiece or tied onto grapevine wreaths.

Ghostly Parfaits

A fun treat for kids.

2 3.9-oz. pkgs. instant
   chocolate pudding mix
3-1/2 c. cold milk
12-oz. container whipped
   topping

16-oz. pkg. chocolate sandwich cookies, crushed
15 8-oz. clear plastic cups
mini chocolate chips and
   candy corn

Make pudding as directed on package, using the milk. Stir in 3 cups of the whipped topping and half of the crushed cookies. Layer pudding and remaining crushed cookies in cups. Top with large ghost-shaped dollops of whipped topping. Make eyes, nose and mouth with mini chips and decorate with candy corn. Makes 5 servings.

This year, invent new designs for your Jack-'O-Lanterns by using Halloween cookie cutters. Trace around the cutters with a marker, then cut out your shapes. Try stacking 3 different sizes of pumpkins on top of one another to make a pumpkin totem.

Witch's Brew

Serve it up in a cauldron for spooky parties!

1/2 c. red-hot cinnamon
   candies
1/2 c. lemon juice
1 qt. apple juice

3 T. brown sugar
6 whole cloves
Garnish: 2 red apples, cored
   and sliced into rings

In a heavy saucepan, melt candies in lemon juice over low heat,
stirring frequently. Add apple juice, brown sugar and cloves.
Simmer for 15 minutes. Remove cloves and pour into punch
bowl or cauldron. Garnish with apple rings. May be served hot
or iced. Makes 10 servings.

Clever tricks & little treats...

Jack-'O-Lantern Lollipop Treat

Decorate your Jack-'O-Lantern, then outline a place for his hair. Drill lots of small holes into the pumpkin's head where the hair would be. Then stick colorful lollipops into the holes. Your pumpkin suddenly has a funny hairdo! A great treat for an elementary school Halloween party. Let the kids pick a lollipop treat from the pumpkin's head.

Popcorn Wreath

Greet goblins and visitors alike with this fun popcorn wreath for your door. Pop 2 unsalted bags of microwave popcorn (or 3 if you want to munch!) and pour onto a baking sheet. Cover a small section of a straw wreath with hot glue and press the popcorn into it. Repeat gluing and pressing the popcorn into the wreath until the entire wreath is covered. Tie a big raffia or orange and black bow to the top of the wreath, and attach a whimsical cut-out (a wicked witch, pumpkin or black cat) to dangle from the center ribbons. After Halloween, remove the ribbons and hang your wreath on a tree limb...welcome treats for squirrels and sparrows!

Pumpkin Cookie Pops

Bake pumpkin-shaped cookies and insert wooden pop sticks into the cookies before baking. Decorate, then wrap each cookie pop with plastic wrap and finish with curly orange ribbon.

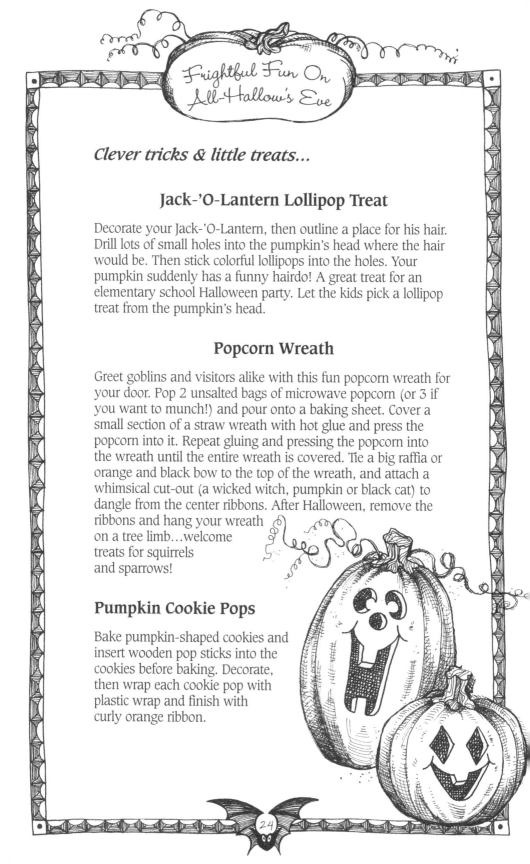

Haunted House Hunt

A spooky older kids' party game: Put objects around a room that are scary to the touch. Use torn cotton balls for spiders' webs, olives in a glass of water for eyeballs, an oak leaf for a bat's wing, a pickle for a witch's nose and chicken bones for a skeleton. Let one person at a time wear a blindfold and lead him around to explore the haunted room, telling him what he's touching: this is the spider's nest; this is the witch's nose, etc. See if he can guess what the objects really are; have a special Halloween treat as the prize. Don't forget to play spooky music!

Roasted Pumpkin Seeds

Save fresh pumpkin seeds from your Jack-'O-Lantern. Coat them in a little vegetable oil and a sprinkling of salt, then bake in a 350-degree oven for about 10 minutes. You can make a sweet variation of this crunchy treat by coating the seeds in butter, brown sugar and cinnamon.

Come for Soup

French Onion Soup with Toasted Rye & Gruyere

Sweet, tender onions in a rich broth, smothered under a canopy of crusty bread and melted cheese.

4 T. butter
4 large sweet onions, halved
and thinly sliced
1/4 c. sugar
salt and pepper to taste

3 16-oz. cans beef broth
Optional: 2 T. sherry
4 thick slices rye bread,
toasted
1 c. Grùyere cheese, grated

Melt the butter in a large soup pot. Cook onions, covered, over low heat for 20 minutes, stirring occasionally. When onions are soft and transparent, sprinkle sugar over them and stir. Continue cooking, uncovered, about 10 minutes, or until onions are brown and caramelized. Add salt and pepper to taste. Add half of the broth and simmer, uncovered, 15 minutes. Add remaining broth and sherry, if using; cook another 30 to 40 minutes. Fill 4 oven-proof soup bowls and put a slice of toasted rye bread on top of each. Divide the cheese among the bowls, sprinkling on top of the bread. Place soup bowls on a baking sheet under a preheated broiler; broil just until cheese melts. Serves 4.

Of soup and love, the first is best.
–Spanish Proverb

Vegetable Stew

A hearty, satisfying way to eat your vegetables.

3 slices bacon
4 T. butter
1-1/2 c. onion, chopped
4 c. leeks, sliced
6 c. chicken broth
2 carrots, sliced
3 stalks celery, sliced
1 t. dried tarragon

1/2 t. dried thyme
salt and pepper to taste
4 c. potatoes, peeled and
    chopped
1 lb. spinach, chopped and
    divided
1/2 c. whipping cream

In a large soup pot, cook bacon over medium-high heat until crisp. Remove bacon and set aside. Lower the heat and add butter. Add onions and leeks to the pot; cook until softened. Pour in broth; add carrots, celery, seasonings and potatoes. Simmer, covered, until potatoes are tender, about 20 minutes. Add half the spinach and simmer for another minute. Remove the soup from heat. Place half the soup in a food processor and purée. Return the puréed soup to the pot. Add cream and remaining spinach. Heat through; adjust seasonings if needed. Ladle into bowls and garnish with reserved bacon. Serves 8.

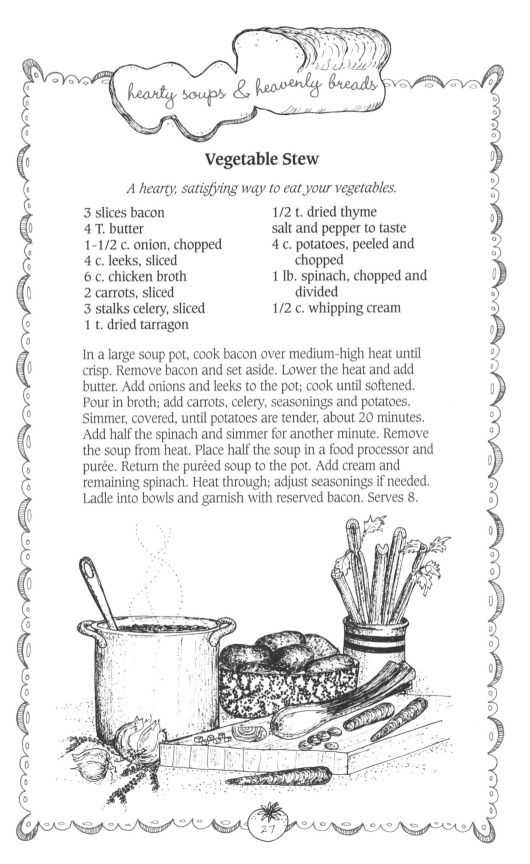

Come for Soup

Mediterranean Peasant Soup

Experiment with different types of day-old bread…garlic, olive or sun-dried tomato.

3 cloves garlic, crushed
1/4 c. olive oil
4 tomatoes, chopped
6 c. beef broth
3 T. fresh basil, chopped

1/8 t. cayenne pepper
salt and pepper to taste
6 thick slices crusty white
    bread, toasted
Garnish: Romano cheese, grated

In a large saucepan sauté garlic in heated olive oil until tender. Add tomatoes and sauté 5 minutes. Add broth and seasonings and bring to a boil. Immediately reduce heat and simmer, covered, about 25 minutes. Break bread into bite-sized pieces and divide among 6 bowls. Pour soup over bread and sprinkle with cheese. Serves 6.

Potato-Cheddar Chowder

The beer adds a hearty malt flavor to this creamy, rich soup.

1/2 c. butter
1 carrot, diced
1 stalk celery, diced
3 scallions, thinly sliced
4 white potatoes, peeled and
   cubed
1/2 c. all-purpose flour
4 c. chicken broth
1-1/2 c. beer or chicken
   broth

1 c. Parmesan cheese, grated
1/2 lb. sharp Cheddar cheese,
   grated
1/2 lb. white Cheddar cheese,
   grated
salt and pepper to taste
Garnish: diced red or green
   pepper, dill weed

In a heavy soup pot, melt the butter over low heat. Add all of
the vegetables and the flour; cook, stirring every so often, for
5 minutes. Add the broth and the beer or broth; simmer,
continuing to stir. With a wire whisk, blend in the cheeses and
the seasonings. Simmer over low heat for about 10 minutes, but
do not boil. Serve in a tureen or individual bowls, garnished
with diced pepper and a sprinkle of dill. Serves 8.

Come for Soup

Burgundy Beef Stew

Fork-tender and richly flavored.

1-1/2 lbs. boneless chuck,
    cut into 1-1/2" cubes
2 T. vegetable oil
2 large baking potatoes, cut
    into 1" cubes
4 large carrots, cut into
    1" slices
1 large turnip, cut into
    1" cubes

2 large onions, chopped
3 T. all-purpose flour
1 c. beef broth
1 c. Burgundy wine or
    beef broth
3 bay leaves
1 t. fresh basil, chopped
Optional: 16-oz. can
    tomatoes, drained

Brown the beef in hot oil in a large stew pot. Add all of the vegetables except the tomatoes; sauté over medium-low heat for about 5 minutes. Sprinkle flour over the meat and vegetables; stir to coat. Add broth, wine or broth, herbs and tomatoes, if using. Bring to a boil and then reduce heat to low. Simmer, covered, for 1-1/2 hours or until meat is very tender, stirring occasionally. Makes 4 to 6 servings.

Italian Wedding Soup

This is the traditional festive soup with little meatballs.

1 lb. ground beef
1 lb. ground sausage
2 eggs
1 c. soft bread crumbs
2 t. dried oregano
1 t. dried rosemary
1 clove garlic, crushed
1 to 2 T. olive oil
2 15-oz. cans chicken broth

2 cans water
5-oz. pkg. vermicelli pasta
1 c. spinach, torn
1 large onion, thinly sliced
6 mushrooms, thinly sliced
2 eggs, lightly beaten
Garnish: Parmesan cheese, grated

In a large bowl, combine beef, sausage, eggs, bread crumbs, oregano, rosemary and garlic. Shape mixture into bite-sized meatballs. Gently brown meatballs in olive oil until cooked; drain. In a large saucepan, combine broth and water and bring to a boil. Add pasta, meatballs, spinach, onion and mushrooms. Simmer, uncovered, until tender. Drop in the eggs, stirring only until eggs are cooked. Remove from heat. Sprinkle individual portions with Parmesan cheese. Serves 10.

Scooped-out round loaves of rye bread make hearty bowls for homemade soups.

Come for Soup

Cream of Broccoli Soup

Indulge by adding a pat of butter to your bowl.

1 large carrot, chopped
1 stalk celery, chopped
1 onion, peeled and chopped
1 potato, peeled and finely
   chopped

4 c. chicken broth
1 large head broccoli, cut in
   flowerets and chopped
1-1/2 c. half-and-half
salt and pepper to taste

Combine all vegetables except the broccoli with the chicken broth in a saucepan and bring to a boil. Reduce heat and simmer, covered, 20 minutes or until tender. Meanwhile, cook the broccoli in another pan or in the microwave until tender. Transfer soup and half the broccoli into a food processor and blend until smooth. Return soup to the pan; blend in the half-and-half and the remaining broccoli. Bring to serving temperature and season with salt and pepper. Serves 8.

Beautiful soup, so rich and green,
Waiting in a hot tureen!
Who for such dainties
would not stoop?
Soup of the evening,
beautiful soup!
   -Lewis Carroll,
   Alice in Wonderland

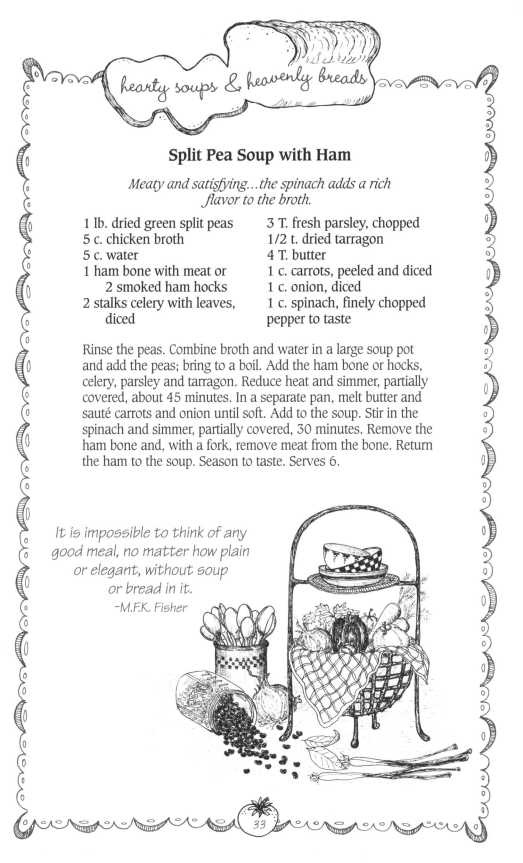

Split Pea Soup with Ham

*Meaty and satisfying...the spinach adds a rich
flavor to the broth.*

1 lb. dried green split peas
5 c. chicken broth
5 c. water
1 ham bone with meat or
    2 smoked ham hocks
2 stalks celery with leaves,
    diced

3 T. fresh parsley, chopped
1/2 t. dried tarragon
4 T. butter
1 c. carrots, peeled and diced
1 c. onion, diced
1 c. spinach, finely chopped
pepper to taste

Rinse the peas. Combine broth and water in a large soup pot
and add the peas; bring to a boil. Add the ham bone or hocks,
celery, parsley and tarragon. Reduce heat and simmer, partially
covered, about 45 minutes. In a separate pan, melt butter and
sauté carrots and onion until soft. Add to the soup. Stir in the
spinach and simmer, partially covered, 30 minutes. Remove the
ham bone and, with a fork, remove meat from the bone. Return
the ham to the soup. Season to taste. Serves 6.

*It is impossible to think of any
good meal, no matter how plain
or elegant, without soup
or bread in it.*
-M.F.K. Fisher

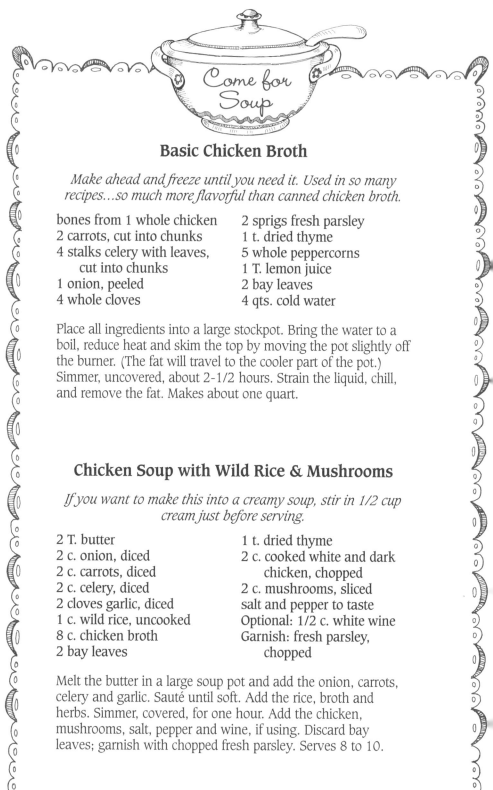

Come for Soup

Basic Chicken Broth

Make ahead and freeze until you need it. Used in so many recipes...so much more flavorful than canned chicken broth.

bones from 1 whole chicken
2 carrots, cut into chunks
4 stalks celery with leaves,
    cut into chunks
1 onion, peeled
4 whole cloves

2 sprigs fresh parsley
1 t. dried thyme
5 whole peppercorns
1 T. lemon juice
2 bay leaves
4 qts. cold water

Place all ingredients into a large stockpot. Bring the water to a boil, reduce heat and skim the top by moving the pot slightly off the burner. (The fat will travel to the cooler part of the pot.) Simmer, uncovered, about 2-1/2 hours. Strain the liquid, chill, and remove the fat. Makes about one quart.

Chicken Soup with Wild Rice & Mushrooms

If you want to make this into a creamy soup, stir in 1/2 cup cream just before serving.

2 T. butter
2 c. onion, diced
2 c. carrots, diced
2 c. celery, diced
2 cloves garlic, diced
1 c. wild rice, uncooked
8 c. chicken broth
2 bay leaves

1 t. dried thyme
2 c. cooked white and dark
    chicken, chopped
2 c. mushrooms, sliced
salt and pepper to taste
Optional: 1/2 c. white wine
Garnish: fresh parsley,
    chopped

Melt the butter in a large soup pot and add the onion, carrots, celery and garlic. Sauté until soft. Add the rice, broth and herbs. Simmer, covered, for one hour. Add the chicken, mushrooms, salt, pepper and wine, if using. Discard bay leaves; garnish with chopped fresh parsley. Serves 8 to 10.

New England Clam Chowder

A basket of crispy oyster crackers is the traditional accompaniment to this hearty favorite.

2 T. all-purpose flour
1 c. milk
2 10-oz. cans baby clams in juice

2 8-oz. bottles clam juice
1 lb. new potatoes, peeled, boiled and cubed

Dissolve the flour in the milk and set aside. In a medium saucepan, combine clams, clam juice and potatoes. Simmer over medium-high heat. Gradually add the milk mixture, stirring constantly, and bring to a boil. Stir for about 3 minutes until soup thickens. Serve immediately. Makes 4 servings.

Only the pure of heart can make a good soup.
-Ludwig Van Beethoven

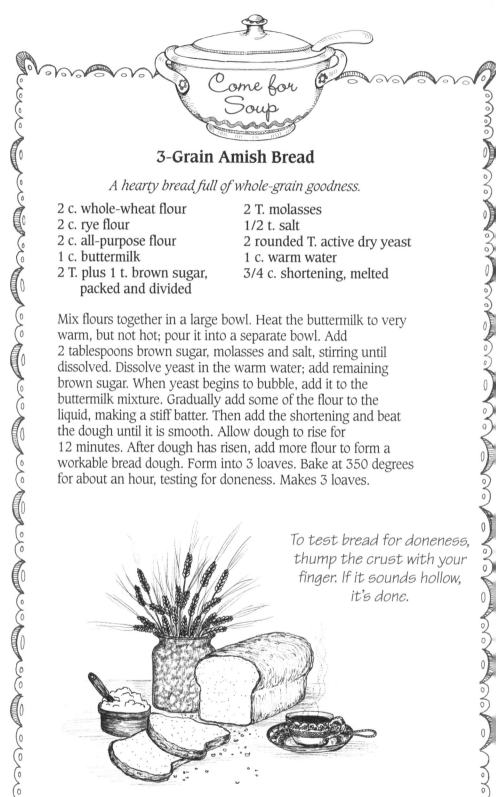

3-Grain Amish Bread

A hearty bread full of whole-grain goodness.

2 c. whole-wheat flour
2 c. rye flour
2 c. all-purpose flour
1 c. buttermilk
2 T. plus 1 t. brown sugar,
   packed and divided

2 T. molasses
1/2 t. salt
2 rounded T. active dry yeast
1 c. warm water
3/4 c. shortening, melted

Mix flours together in a large bowl. Heat the buttermilk to very warm, but not hot; pour it into a separate bowl. Add 2 tablespoons brown sugar, molasses and salt, stirring until dissolved. Dissolve yeast in the warm water; add remaining brown sugar. When yeast begins to bubble, add it to the buttermilk mixture. Gradually add some of the flour to the liquid, making a stiff batter. Then add the shortening and beat the dough until it is smooth. Allow dough to rise for 12 minutes. After dough has risen, add more flour to form a workable bread dough. Form into 3 loaves. Bake at 350 degrees for about an hour, testing for doneness. Makes 3 loaves.

To test bread for doneness, thump the crust with your finger. If it sounds hollow, it's done.

Cheddar Cheese Spoon Bread

A delicious companion to soup or chowder.

2-1/4 c. water
1 t. salt
1 c. cornmeal
1/2 t. pepper
1 T. butter

1 c. milk
4 large eggs, well beaten
1-1/2 c. sharp Cheddar
    cheese, shredded
3 T. scallions, chopped

Bring water to a boil in a large saucepan. Add salt and lower heat to simmering. Add the cornmeal while stirring with a wire whisk and continue to cook, stirring constantly, for about 2 minutes or until mixture is smooth. Remove from heat and whisk in pepper, butter and milk. When mixture is smooth, add the eggs and beat with the whisk. Stir in cheese and scallions. Pour the mixture into a buttered 2-quart casserole and bake at 400 degrees for 40 minutes, or until a toothpick comes out clean. Serves 6 to 8.

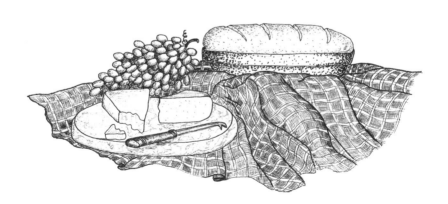

Before the introduction of coins, the Egyptians gave loaves of bread as payment for their debts. (This gave new meaning to the word "dough"!)

Crusty Cornmeal Rolls

*A delicious roll that's worth the time...prepare a good
vegetable soup while you're waiting for the dough to rise!*

1/3 c. cornmeal	2 eggs, beaten
1/2 c. sugar	1 pkg. active dry yeast
1 t. salt	1/4 c. lukewarm water
1/2 c. shortening, melted	4 c. all-purpose flour
2 c. milk	3 T. butter, melted

In a double boiler, combine cornmeal, sugar, salt, shortening
and milk. Stir the mixture often, cooking until it is thick. Allow
to cool, then add the eggs. Dissolve the yeast in water and add
to batter. Beat well, then allow to rise in a greased bowl for
about 2 hours. After batter has risen, add the flour to form a soft
dough. Knead the dough lightly, and allow to rise again for
another hour. Then knead again. Roll the dough out with a
floured rolling pin and cut into rounds with a biscuit cutter.
Brush with butter, then with floured hands, fold into desired
shapes (fans, twists, rolls, etc.). Place on a greased baking sheet
and allow to rise for another hour. Then bake at 375 degrees for
just 15 minutes or so. Makes 3 dozen rolls.

I never had a piece of toast
Particularly long and wide,
But fell upon the sanded floor,
And always on the buttered side.

-James Payn

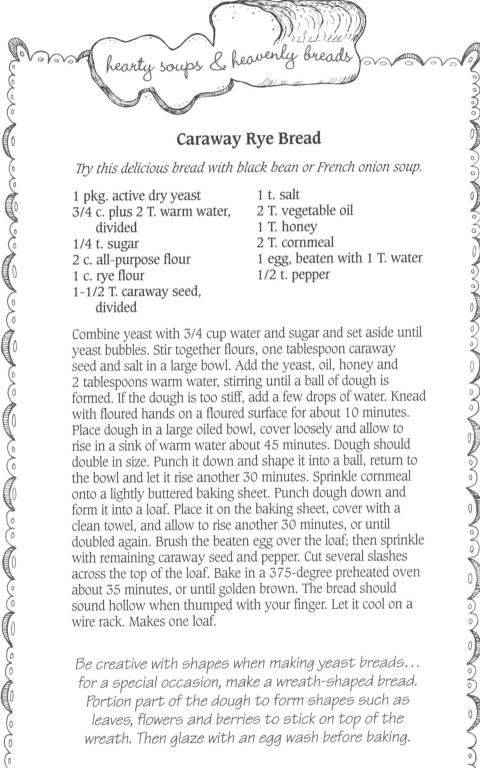

Caraway Rye Bread

Try this delicious bread with black bean or French onion soup.

1 pkg. active dry yeast	1 t. salt
3/4 c. plus 2 T. warm water, divided	2 T. vegetable oil
1/4 t. sugar	1 T. honey
2 c. all-purpose flour	2 T. cornmeal
1 c. rye flour	1 egg, beaten with 1 T. water
1-1/2 T. caraway seed, divided	1/2 t. pepper

Combine yeast with 3/4 cup water and sugar and set aside until yeast bubbles. Stir together flours, one tablespoon caraway seed and salt in a large bowl. Add the yeast, oil, honey and 2 tablespoons warm water, stirring until a ball of dough is formed. If the dough is too stiff, add a few drops of water. Knead with floured hands on a floured surface for about 10 minutes. Place dough in a large oiled bowl, cover loosely and allow to rise in a sink of warm water about 45 minutes. Dough should double in size. Punch it down and shape it into a ball, return to the bowl and let it rise another 30 minutes. Sprinkle cornmeal onto a lightly buttered baking sheet. Punch dough down and form it into a loaf. Place it on the baking sheet, cover with a clean towel, and allow to rise another 30 minutes, or until doubled again. Brush the beaten egg over the loaf; then sprinkle with remaining caraway seed and pepper. Cut several slashes across the top of the loaf. Bake in a 375-degree preheated oven about 35 minutes, or until golden brown. The bread should sound hollow when thumped with your finger. Let it cool on a wire rack. Makes one loaf.

Be creative with shapes when making yeast breads… for a special occasion, make a wreath-shaped bread. Portion part of the dough to form shapes such as leaves, flowers and berries to stick on top of the wreath. Then glaze with an egg wash before baking.

Ripe Olive Bread

They'll think you spent the day baking this quick, easy bread!

2 eggs
1 T. sugar
1/2 t. salt
1/4 c. olive oil

1/2 c. milk
1 c. black olives, chopped
1 c. all-purpose flour
2 t. baking soda

In a large bowl, beat eggs, sugar, salt, oil and milk. Add olives. Stir together the flour and baking soda and add to egg mixture, stirring just until blended. Do not overbeat. Pour into a greased 9"x5" loaf pan. Bake at 350 degrees for about one hour, or until a toothpick comes out clean. Remove loaf from pan after it has cooled for 10 minutes and allow to cool completely. Makes one loaf.

Little Bread Cups

Fun to serve on the side...fill with soup garnishes such as cheese, croutons, fresh chives and sour cream.

12 slices white bread
3 T. olive oil

fresh herbs of your choice

Trim crusts from the bread and flatten with a rolling pin. Press flattened bread slices into the cups of a muffin tin, trimming excess bread with a sharp knife. Brush each bread cup with olive oil. Sprinkle with dill, parsley, tarragon or garlic powder. Bake in a preheated 425-degree oven for about 10 minutes, or until crisp. Allow to cool for a few minutes before removing from muffin tin. Makes one dozen.

Without bread,
without wine,
love is nothing.
-French proverb

Ideas to bowl them over...

Try serving soups and chowders in these creative containers!

Butternut squash...just cut in half, remove seeds and fibers, and cook in the microwave.

Bell peppers make lovely soup cups. Make sure you select peppers that will stand up. If you like, vary the colors of red, green and yellow. After you remove the seeds and membranes, fill the raw peppers and replace the tops to keep the soup hot.

Little rye or sourdough bread rounds can be scooped out and brushed with olive oil. Brown in a 350-degree oven about 10 minutes, then fill the loaves. Garnish with croutons made from the leftover bread.

Special Soup Garnishes:

Toasted nuts
Paprika
Cooked, crumbled bacon
Slices or zest of lemon or
  lime
Sour cream
Matchstick carrots

Diced green onions
Paper-thin pepper rings
Tortilla chips
Rye, sourdough or whole-
  wheat herbed croutons
Shredded cheese
Fresh parsley or dill

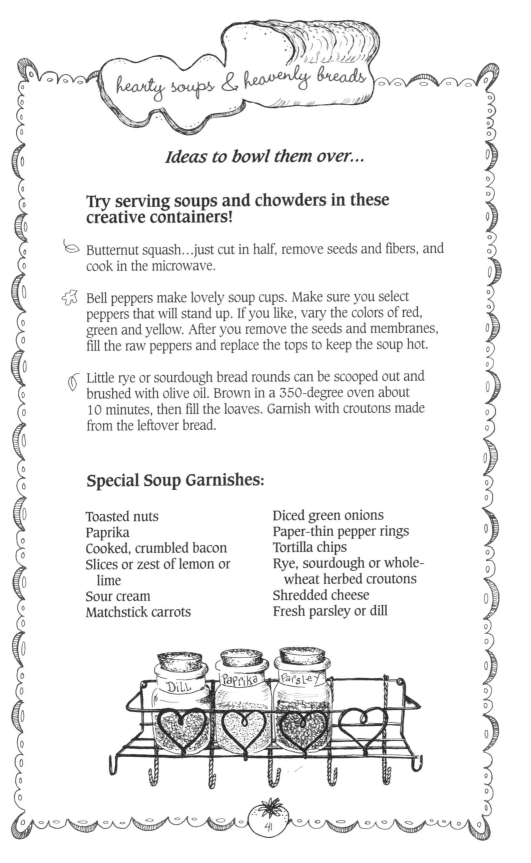

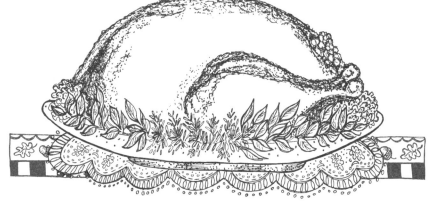

Sage-Roasted Turkey

Bursting with fragrant juices...a Thanksgiving triumph!

12 to 14-lb. turkey
1/2 t. salt
1/2 t. pepper

1 bunch fresh sage leaves
1/2 c. butter, melted

Remove giblets and neck from turkey; set aside. Rinse turkey under running water; drain well and pat dry thoroughly with paper towels. Sprinkle inside and out with salt and pepper. Gently loosen skin; arrange as many sage leaves as desired under the skin. Pat skin back into place. Loosely stuff neck and body with stuffing, if desired. Close both openings with skewers. Tie legs together; tuck wings under body. Place turkey, breast-side up, on a rack in a shallow roasting pan. Brush all over with melted butter. Roast 15 minutes at 425 degrees; reduce temperature to 325 degrees. Roast 4 to 4-1/2 hours or longer, continuing to baste with drippings, until breast skin is crisp and golden and juices run clear when thigh is pricked with fork. If turkey is browning too quickly, it may be covered loosely with foil. Meat thermometer should register 180 degrees. Serves 12 to 14.

...a bounty of savory traditional fare

Cornbread Stuffing with Sage & Sausage

Use mild sausage and thyme, if you prefer.

8" square day-old cornbread
1 lb. sweet Italian sausage
2 small onions, finely
    chopped
6 stalks celery, finely
    chopped
2 cloves garlic, minced

Optional: 1/2 c. pine nuts,
    toasted
1 T. dried sage
1 c. chicken broth
4 T. butter, melted
salt and pepper to taste

Cut cornbread into 1/2-inch cubes and spread evenly on a baking sheet. Toast in 350-degree oven about 20 minutes, or until golden. Heat a large skillet over medium-high heat and brown sausage 6 to 8 minutes, until brown. Drain, reserving one teaspoon of fat in the pan. Add onions to skillet and cook until translucent. Add celery and garlic and cook until celery is soft. Combine sausage, onion mixture, cornbread, pine nuts and sage in a large bowl and mix well. Add chicken broth and melted butter and toss to combine. Season with salt and pepper to taste. Allow to cool before stuffing turkey. Makes 10 cups, enough to stuff a 14-pound turkey with some left over for a separate baking dish.

Baked squash is delicious stuffed with sausage dressing or raisins and chopped apples. Try a little cooked, crumbled bacon on top. Yum!

Scalloped Oysters

A New England tradition.

3 pts. oysters, drained and
    liquid reserved
2 c. coarse cracker crumbs

1/2 c. butter, melted
salt and pepper to taste
3/4 c. milk

Check each oyster for shells and remove. Put one layer of cracker crumbs and one layer of oysters in a well-buttered casserole. Sprinkle with salt and pepper and drizzle butter over the top. Continue to layer oysters, crumbs, seasonings and butter, ending with cracker crumbs. Mix oyster liquid and milk. Pour over top of casserole. Drizzle with remaining butter. Bake, uncovered, at 375 degrees for 30 to 40 minutes. Serves 6 to 8.

Thanksgiving originated as 3 days of prayer and feasting celebrated in 1621 by the Plymouth colonists. In 1863, President Abraham Lincoln declared Thanksgiving an annual holiday to be celebrated on the last Thursday in November. The Thanksgiving menu hasn't changed much from the original one of roast turkey, stuffing, cranberry sauce and pumpkin pie. These are the main dishes of the New England harvest home feast, and have remained favorites to this day.

Stuffed Roast Duck

This is a little different way to prepare duck. It is very moist and flavorful!

4-lb. duck   32-oz. pkg. sauerkraut
salt and pepper to taste

Remove giblets and neck from duck; set aside. Rinse thoroughly inside and out. Dry well with paper towels. Season inside with salt and pepper. Stuff neck and body loosely with sauerkraut. Place on rack in a shallow pan. Prick the skin several times. Bake at 325 degrees for 2-1/2 hours. For a colorful garnish, add vegetables such as carrots, onions and Brussels sprouts to roasting pan during last 40 minutes of cooking. Serves 4 to 6.

The maple wears a gayer scarf,
The field a scarlet gown.
Lest I should be old-fashioned,
I'll put a trinket on.
-Emily Dickinson

Herbed Mashed Potatoes

These can be made with either sour cream or cream cheese. Delicious!

6-1/2 c. baking potatoes, peeled and cubed
2 cloves garlic, halved
1/2 c. milk
1/2 c. sour cream
2 T. fresh parsley, minced

2 T. fresh oregano, minced
1 T. fresh thyme, minced
1 T. butter
3/4 t. salt
1/8 t. pepper

Cover potatoes and garlic with water in a large saucepan; bring to a boil. Simmer 20 minutes, or until very tender; drain. Return potatoes to pan. Add remaining ingredients; beat at medium speed with an electric mixer until smooth. Serves 6.

Scalloped Sweet Potatoes

A hearty family favorite.

4 lbs. sweet potatoes, peeled
   and sliced lengthwise
3-1/2 c. milk
salt and pepper to taste

1 c. light brown sugar,
   packed
1/4 c. butter, diced

In heavy saucepan, combine sweet potatoes with milk and bring to a boil over moderate heat. Add salt and pepper. Transfer mixture to a greased 14-inch gratin dish and bake, covered, in a 400-degree oven for 20 minutes. Reduce heat to 350 degrees and bake, covered, 20 minutes more. Sprinkle potatoes with brown sugar and dot with butter. Bake, uncovered, 10 minutes longer. Serves 8.

Hurrah for the fun!
Is the turkey done?
Hurrah for the pumpkin pie!
-Lydia Maria Child

Remembering Thanksgiving

Fresh Cranberry Ring

Beautiful served on a cut-glass plate with cool green grapes.

2 c. cranberries
1/2 t. lemon zest
3/4 c. sugar
1/2 c. cold water
2 envs. unflavored gelatin

1 c. red wine or white grape
  juice
1/2 c. walnuts, chopped
2 T. lemon juice
1/2 c. mayonnaise

Chop cranberries in a blender or food processor; stir in lemon zest and sugar, and set aside in a bowl. Pour cold water in the blender and sprinkle gelatin on the water. Allow to soften 10 minutes. Heat wine or grape juice to a almost boiling and add to the blender. Blend unti gelatin has dissolved. Mix cranberries, walnuts, lemon juice and mayonnaise with the gelatin mixture and pour into a wet 1-1/2 quart ring mold. Refrigerate until set. Serves 8.

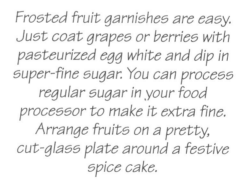

Frosted fruit garnishes are easy. Just coat grapes or berries with pasteurized egg white and dip in super-fine sugar. You can process regular sugar in your food processor to make it extra fine. Arrange fruits on a pretty, cut-glass plate around a festive spice cake.

Broccoli with Orange Sauce

Good old broccoli...all dressed up for the holidays.

1 lb. broccoli, cut into
   spears
2 T. butter
1 T. cornstarch
1 c. orange juice, divided
1 T. fresh parsley, minced
1 T. lemon juice

1 T. orange zest
1/2 t. dried thyme
1/2 t. dry mustard
1/4 t. pepper
Garnish: orange slices or
   orange zest

Steam broccoli just until tender. In separate saucepan, melt butter. Blend in cornstarch and 1/2 cup orange juice, stirring until blended. Mix in remaining orange juice and other ingredients except garnish. Cook over moderate heat until mixture thickens. Pour over broccoli. Garnish with thin slices of orange or slivers of orange zest. Serves 4.

The golden-rod is yellow.
The corn is turning brown:
The trees in apple orchards
With fruit are bending down.
    -Helen Hunt Jackson

Maple Indian Pudding

A traditional fall dessert from Grandmother's time.

1 c. cornmeal
1 qt. milk
1/2 c. brown sugar, packed

1 c. whipping cream
1/2 c. pure maple syrup
1/8 t. nutmeg

Butter a 1-1/2 quart soufflé dish. In heavy saucepan, whisk cornmeal into the milk over moderately high heat, stirring until slightly thickened, about 5 minutes. Remove from heat and stir in the brown sugar. Add cream, maple syrup and nutmeg. Pour in the prepared dish and bake in a 275-degree oven about 4 hours, until pudding is bubbly and top is brown. Allow to rest 30 minutes before serving. Serves 6 to 8.

For pottage and puddings and custards and pies
Our pumpkins and parsnips are common supplies;
We have pumpkin at morning and pumpkin at noon,
If it was not for pumpkin, we should be undone.
-Colonial rhyme

Spicy Pumpkin Pie

It wouldn't be Thanksgiving without a pumpkin pie!

2-1/4 c. all-purpose flour
1/2 t. salt
1/2 c. cold butter, diced
3 T. cold shortening
4 to 5 T. ice water, divided
Garnish: whipped cream

Combine flour and salt in a food processor and pulse a few times to mix. Add butter and shortening and process until the mixture is textured with pea-size particles. Add 3 tablespoons ice water, one tablespoon at a time, pulsing briefly after each addition. Add another tablespoon of water and pulse until the dough begins to hold together. Add the last tablespoon of water only if necessary. Place dough on a lightly floured surface and gather into a ball, handling it as little as possible. Divide dough in half; pat into 2 disks, wrap in wax paper and refrigerate for at least 30 minutes. Roll into 2 rounds and fit into 9" pie pans, fitting against bottoms and sides of pans without stretching. Trim excess dough to about 1/2 inch; fold it under and crimp or press into a pattern. Prick dough all over with a fork; freeze crusts for 30 minutes. In a preheated 375-degree oven, bake crusts for 10 minutes, or until they begin to brown slightly. Allow to cool to room temperature. Pour Pumpkin Pie Filling into cooled crusts and bake for about 45 minutes, until pies move very slightly in one mass when lightly jiggled. Transfer to a rack for cooling. Serve with plenty of freshly whipped cream. Makes 2 pies.

Pumpkin Pie Filling:

29-oz. can solid-pack
   pumpkin
2 c. light brown sugar,
   packed
3 T. pumpkin pie spice
1 t. salt
5 large eggs, lightly beaten
2 12-oz. cans evaporated
   milk

In a large bowl, whisk together pumpkin, brown sugar, spice and salt. Whisk in eggs. Slowly whisk in evaporated milk until completely blended. Chill thoroughly.

Making it memorable...

Marinated Olives

These olives are quite spicy and will please anyone who loves to nibble on hot foods! Take one jar each of pitted black olives and pitted green olives. Empty them into a sieve and rinse thoroughly in cold water. Set aside. Take a hot chili pepper and 3 cloves of garlic and mince them very fine. Add a teaspoon of oregano. Then put everything into a jar and cover with olive oil; refrigerate. Shake your olives gently for a minute or so each week. After a few weeks, your olives will be ready for company.

Herb Candles

Gather fresh bay leaves, parsley, tarragon, basil or any combination of your favorite herbs. Select a large, white or ivory pillar candle. You will need a heat-proof container that is taller and wider than the candle. Fill the container with enough hot water to reach the shoulder of the candle when it is immersed. Holding the candle by the wick, immerse it in the hot water for about 30 seconds. Remove the candle and press your herbs onto the softened wax. Refill the container with more very hot water and dip the candle again briefly to seal in the herbs.

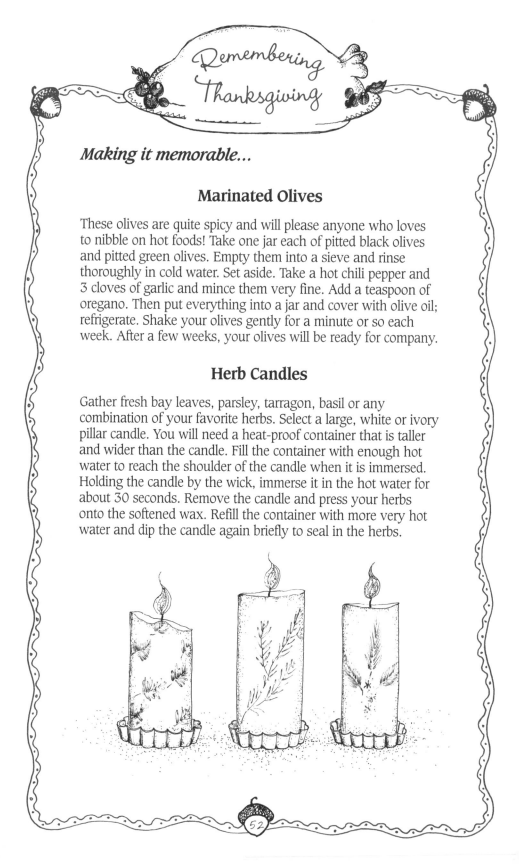

Celebrate Winter

Cozy Winter Warmers

Cranberry Hot Toddies

It's sure to warm you to your toes!

16-oz. can jellied cranberry
   sauce
1/3 c. light brown sugar,
   packed
1/4 t. cinnamon
1/4 t. allspice

1/8 t. nutmeg
1/8 t. ground cloves
1/8 t. salt
2 c. water
2 c. pineapple juice
2 T. butter, sliced

Empty cranberry sauce into a large pan. Whisk in sugar and
seasonings; add water and pineapple juice. Cover and allow to
simmer for about 2 hours. Pour into mugs and top each mug
with a pat of butter. Serves 6 to 8.

welcome
recipes for rosy
winter cheeks

Cinnamon Hot Chocolate

Both grownups and kids will love this chill-chaser.

1/4 c. baking cocoa
1/4 c. sugar
1 c. boiling water

3 c. milk
1 cinnamon stick
1 t. vanilla extract

In a double boiler, combine cocoa and sugar. Slowly add in boiling water; bring to a boil for 2 minutes; add milk and cinnamon stick. Reduce heat; simmer for 10 minutes. Remove cinnamon stick and add vanilla; stir quickly to froth milk. Serves 4.

Jack Frost Warm-Up

A warm apple drink that goes well with gingerbread!

1 qt. apple cider
1/4 c. brown sugar, packed
5 whole cloves

1 cinnamon stick
Garnish: orange slices,
   whipped cream, nutmeg

Heat cider, brown sugar, cloves and cinnamon stick slowly over low heat in a 2-quart saucepan for 20 minutes. Remove spices. Serve warm, garnished as desired. Serves 4.

Make your favorite hot chocolate extra special. Add a scoop of vanilla ice cream. Then top with whipped cream and dust with cocoa powder. Add a cinnamon stick and sprinkle some chocolate curls on top. Totally yummy!

Hot Jalapeño Poppers

A favorite appetizer for those who love a bit of heat.

16 whole preserved jalapeño
  peppers
1 lb. cream cheese, softened

1 egg, beaten
1 c. bread crumbs
4 T. vegetable oil

Open the end of each pepper with a small knife to remove the stem and seeds. Using a pastry tube or small sandwich bag with one corner cut off, fill each pepper with cream cheese; coat peppers in the egg and bread crumbs. Heat oil in a large sauté pan over medium heat; carefully place peppers in the pan and sauté until coating is browned and peppers are heated through, turning occasionally. Drain on paper towels. Serves 4.

While the grownups are visiting, set up a holiday activity just for kids. Arrange a cloth around the Christmas tree, complete with big bowls of popcorn and cranberries for stringing.

Creamy Crab Bisque

This is one of the richest we've tried!

1 c. crabmeat, cleaned and
    chopped
10-3/4 oz. can cream of
    mushroom soup
10-3/4 oz. can cream of
    asparagus soup

1 c. light cream
1-1/4 c. milk
1/2 t. Worcestershire sauce
1 t. hot pepper sauce
Garnish: oyster crackers

In a heavy saucepan, mix together crabmeat and soups. Add remaining ingredients and heat thoroughly. Serve in soup mugs with oyster crackers alongside. Serves 4.

Winter is the time for comfort,
for good food and warmth,
for the touch of a friendly hand and for a
talk beside the fire;
it is the time for home.
-Edith Sitwell

Chocolate Mint Brownies

Be sure to make plenty...these won't last long!

4 sqs. unsweetened
    chocolate, divided
3/4 c. butter, divided
1 c. sugar
2 eggs, beaten
1/2 c. all-purpose flour

1 c. powdered sugar
cream or milk
peppermint extract to taste
green food coloring to
    desired color

Melt 2 squares chocolate with 1/2 cup butter. Remove from heat; stir in sugar. Add eggs and mix again. Blend in flour and mix well. Pour into a greased 13"x9" baking pan; bake at 350 degrees for 15 minutes. Prepare frosting by combining powdered sugar, 2 tablespoons butter, cream to desired consistency, peppermint extract and green food coloring. Spread frosting on brownies; refrigerate for one hour. Melt remaining chocolate with remaining butter; drizzle over green frosting. Refrigerate 30 minutes; cut into squares when firm. Makes 2 dozen.

The smell of buttered toast simply talked to Toad, and with no uncertain voice; talked of warm kitchens, of breakfasts on bright frosty mornings, of cosy parlour firesides on winter evenings, when one's ramble was over and slippered feet were propped on the fender; of the purring of contented cats, and the twitter of sleepy canaries.
    –Kenneth Grahame,
    The Wind in the Willows

Warm Sweet Potato Muffins

Set them out with hot drinks and watch them disappear.

1-1/4 c. sugar
1-1/4 c. canned sweet
   potatoes, mashed
1/2 c. butter, softened
2 large eggs, room
   temperature
1-1/2 c. all-purpose
   flour
2 t. baking powder

1 t. cinnamon
1/4 t. nutmeg
1/4 t. salt
1 c. milk
1/2 c. raisins, chopped
1/4 c. walnuts, chopped
2 T. sugar and 1/4 t.
   cinnamon, mixed
   together

Line 24 muffin cups with paper liners. Preheat oven to
400 degrees. Beat together sugar, sweet potatoes and butter until
smooth. Add eggs and blend well. Sift together flour, baking
powder, spices and salt. Add to sweet potato mixture, alternating
with the milk, and stirring to blend. Do not overmix. Fold in
raisins and nuts. Fill muffin cups three-quarters full; sprinkle each
muffin with sugar and cinnamon mixture. Bake for 25 to
30 minutes, or until muffins test done with a toothpick. Serve
warm. Makes 2 dozen.

Cake Stencils

Stencil holiday designs onto your chocolate cakes, coffee cakes and brownies with powdered sugar. Just use heavy paper and sharp scissors to cut out a reindeer, star, Santa or tree shape. Or use your favorite cookie cutter. Sift or shake powdered sugar onto the cake. If you've baked a large sheet cake, you can create a whole Christmas scene with powdered sugar!

Is the paint flaking off of your glass ornaments? Buy glitter, faux jewels or sequins, or use beads from broken costume jewelry to cover the old paint with sparkles and twinkles.

Little Gold Baskets

Tiny willow baskets, available at most craft and import shops, are just right for painting. A light coat of gold spray paint gives them a sheen, yet allows the woven texture to show through. After they've dried, fill them with foil-wrapped milk chocolate drops or coins for good luck. Finish with a gold fabric bow, a tiny pine cone and a sprig of greenery. Hang them on the tree; one for each member of your family.

Little girls love to dress up their dolls. Along with that new doll, give her colorful rolls of fabric remnants, safety scissors and bits of ribbons and lace for making doll fashions. The best part of the gift...spending an afternoon helping her create new styles.

Yuletide Candlelight Dinner

Artichokes with Mustard-Butter Sauce

Take your time savoring this delectable appetizer!

6 whole artichokes
6 T. lemon juice

6 cloves garlic, minced
6 c. water

Trim bottoms of artichokes flat; snip one inch off tops of leaves. Sprinkle lemon juice and garlic between leaves. In a large saucepan with a steamer insert, bring water to a boil over high heat. Set artichokes upright in pan. Cover; steam artichokes until tender, 40 to 45 minutes. Serve with Mustard-Butter Sauce. Serves 6.

Mustard-Butter Sauce:

1 c. dry white wine or
    chicken broth
2 shallots, minced
1 c. whipping cream

1 c. butter, softened
2 T. Dijon mustard
salt and pepper to taste

In a saucepan over low heat, simmer wine or broth and shallots until reduced by half. Add cream; simmer until very thick. Whisk in butter, salt and pepper.

Prime Rib Roast with Yorkshire Pudding

*A glorious roast of prime rib, crusty on the outside,
juicy and pink in the middle, makes the perfect holiday feast.
Yorkshire pudding, steeped in tradition, is an easy recipe that
adds that special touch.*

5-lb. beef prime rib roast,   pepper to taste
   fat trimmed   13-3/4 oz. can beef broth

Place roast on its rib bones in an open roasting pan; sprinkle
with pepper. Roast, uncovered, at 325 degrees for about
1-1/2 hours, until a meat thermometer registers 130 degrees
(rare) to 140 degrees (medium). Remove roast from oven;
raise oven temperature to 400 degrees. Skim fat from pan; add
broth and pour pudding batter around roast. Return roast to
oven for 30 minutes. (Keep an eye on the meat thermometer to
make sure you don't overcook the roast!) Cut pudding into
squares and arrange around roast. Serves 8 to 10.

Yorkshire Pudding:

2 large eggs   1/2 t. salt
1 c. milk   1 c. all-purpose flour

In a mixing bowl, whisk eggs until foamy. Beat in milk and salt;
gradually beat in flour until mixture is smooth.

*Oh! What a wonderful pudding!,
Bob Cratchit said, and calmly too,
that he regarded it as the greatest
success achieved by Mrs. Cratchit
since their marriage.*
-Charles Dickens, A Christmas Carol

Sour Cream Mashed Potatoes

These baked mashed potatoes are an old favorite.

5 lbs. russet or Yukon Gold
   potatoes, peeled and
   cubed
2 T. butter

1 c. sour cream
salt and pepper to taste
4 slices bacon, cooked
   and crumbled

Cover potatoes with cold salted water. Bring to a boil; simmer
for 20 minutes or until tender. Drain and mash with a potato
masher or ricer. Whisk in butter and sour cream; season to taste.
Sprinkle with crumbled bacon. Transfer to a greased baking
dish; bake at 350 degrees for 10 to 15 minutes. Serves 10.

Creamed Onions with Peanuts

This southern dish is full of flavor and crunchy texture.

20 whole small white onions,
   peeled
2 T. butter
2 T. all-purpose flour
2 c. milk

1/4 c. whole salted peanuts
1/2 c. bread crumbs
1/4 c. salted peanuts, coarsely
   chopped

Cook onions in boiling salted water until tender; drain. Melt
butter in a small saucepan and stir in flour. Add milk and cook
over medium heat, stirring until smooth and thickened. Put
onions in a greased 2-quart casserole dish and pour the sauce
over them. Stir in whole peanuts. Top with bread crumbs and
chopped peanuts. Bake at 400 degrees for 15 minutes, or until
lightly browned. Serves 6 to 8.

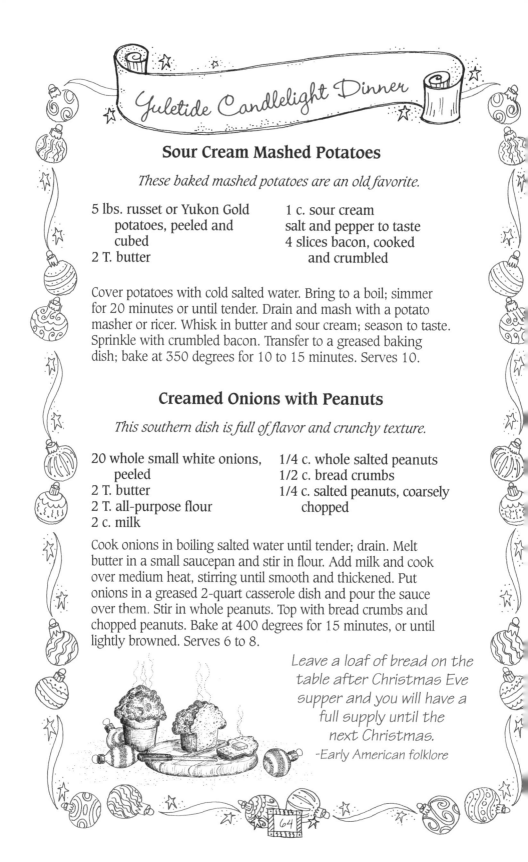

*Leave a loaf of bread on the
table after Christmas Eve
supper and you will have a
full supply until the
next Christmas.*
-Early American folklore

Glazed Carrots

Carrots add a cheerful, bright splash of color and flavor.

2 T. onion, chopped
2 T. parsley, chopped
2 T. butter
8 carrots, peeled and quartered

10-1/2 oz. can beef
  consommé
1/4 t. sugar
Optional: nutmeg

Sauté onion and parsley in butter until tender. Add carrots, consommé and sugar. Cover and cook 5 minutes. Uncover and cook 10 minutes more, or until carrots are crisp-tender. Sprinkle with a little nutmeg if you like. Serves 8.

Pears with Cranberry Relish

A light, refreshing, healthful medley of fruit colors and flavors.

12-oz. pkg. cranberries
2 red apples, unpeeled, cored
  and quartered
1 lemon, unpeeled, quartered
  and seeded

1-1/2 c. sugar
6 Bartlett pears, halved
  lengthwise and cored

In a food processor, process berries, apples and lemon using a medium blade until well chopped. Stir in sugar; cover and chill in refrigerator. Hollow out each pear half with the tip of a spoon. Spoon relish into the pears and serve. Serves 12.

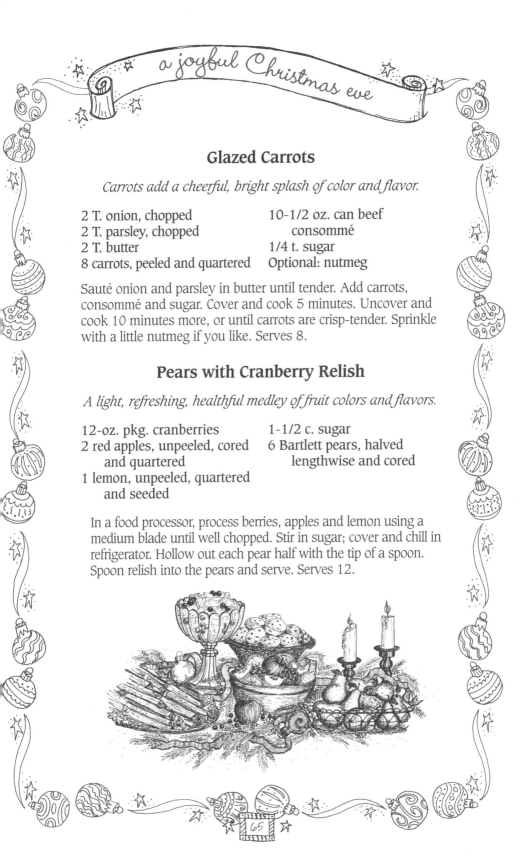

Frozen Christmas Salad

So cool and creamy!

3/4 pkg. miniature
    marshmallows
20-oz. can crushed
    pineapple, drained
1/2 c. mayonnaise
8-oz. pkg. cream cheese

1/2 c. walnuts, chopped
12 ea. red and green
    maraschino cherries,
    chopped
1 c. whipping cream
lettuce leaves

Combine marshmallows and pineapple; set aside until marshmallows are well soaked. Mix mayonnaise and cream cheese and combine with marshmallow mixture. Add chopped cherries and nuts. Whip the whipping cream and fold into the salad. Pour into mold or container of your choice and freeze. Cut into squares and serve on lettuce leaves. Serves 10.

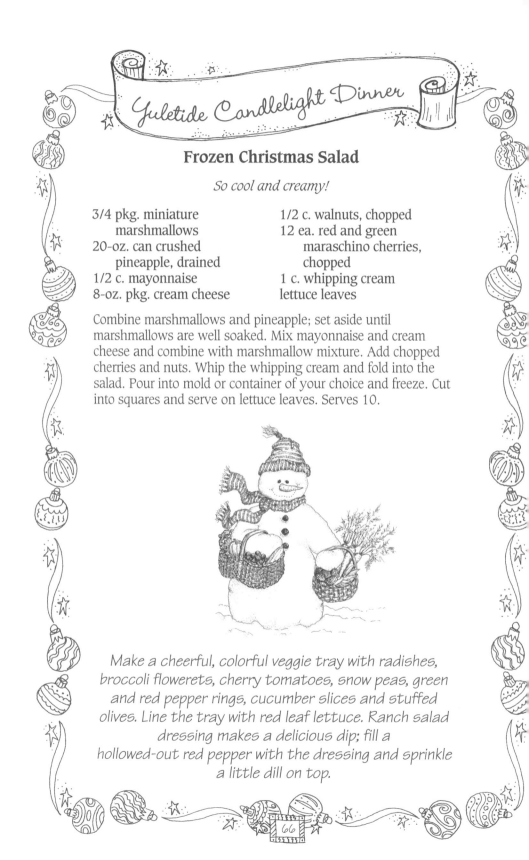

Make a cheerful, colorful veggie tray with radishes, broccoli flowerets, cherry tomatoes, snow peas, green and red pepper rings, cucumber slices and stuffed olives. Line the tray with red leaf lettuce. Ranch salad dressing makes a delicious dip; fill a hollowed-out red pepper with the dressing and sprinkle a little dill on top.

Candied Oranges

A canister of candied oranges makes a lovely hostess gift.

1-1/3 c. sugar
4 c. water
1 T. vanilla extract
1 t. cinnamon
1/2 t. ground nutmeg

6 seedless oranges, skins
   lightly grated to release
   oils
1 c. whipped cream
Optional: 2 T. brandy

Combine sugar, water, vanilla and spices in a large, heavy pan. Bring to a boil, reduce heat to low, cover and simmer for 20 minutes. Add oranges, making sure they are covered about three-quarters of the way up by syrup. Cover and slowly cook oranges for 2 hours, turning a few times during cooking. Remove pan from heat and add lemon juice. Place cover back on pan and refrigerate overnight. To serve, slice oranges into wheels and arrange on a pretty plate. Top with whipped cream, flavored with brandy, if desired. Serves 6.

God bless the master of this house,
*   Likewise the mistress too;*
*   And all the little children*
*   That round the table go.*
*   -English carol*

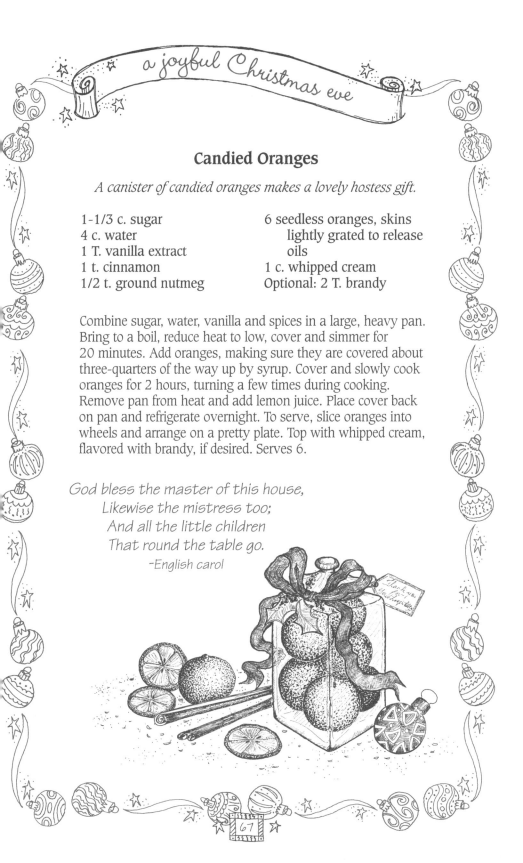

Walnut Torte

*A heavenly combination of walnuts with rich coffee
and a creamy filling.*

8 large eggs, separated
3/4 c. plus 2 T. sugar, divided
1-1/2 c. chopped walnuts
2 T. soft bread crumbs

1 T. strong brewed coffee
2 T. dark rum or 1/2 t. rum
    extract
Garnish: toasted walnuts

Line three, 9" round cake pans with wax paper; butter and flour
the paper. Beat egg yolks with 3/4 cup sugar until double in
volume, about 5 minutes at medium-high with an electric
mixer. Set aside. Grind walnuts with remaining sugar in a food
processor until very fine. Gently fold nuts, crumbs, coffee and
rum or extract into egg yolk mixture. Beat egg whites just until
stiff; fold into egg yolk mixture. Pour into prepared cake pans.
Bake at 350 degrees for about 24 minutes, or until light golden;
cake should spring back when touched with a fingertip. Let cool
about 10 minutes; loosen with a knife and place on a rack,
removing paper. When cake is completely cooled, spread filling
over each layer and garnish with toasted walnuts. Chill one
hour before serving. Serves 12.

Filling:

1-1/2 T. instant coffee powder
1-1/2 c. whipping cream

3/4 c. powdered sugar

Stir coffee into a small amount of the cream
until dissolved. Add remaining
cream and sugar. Beat until
cream is very fluffy and forms
soft peaks.

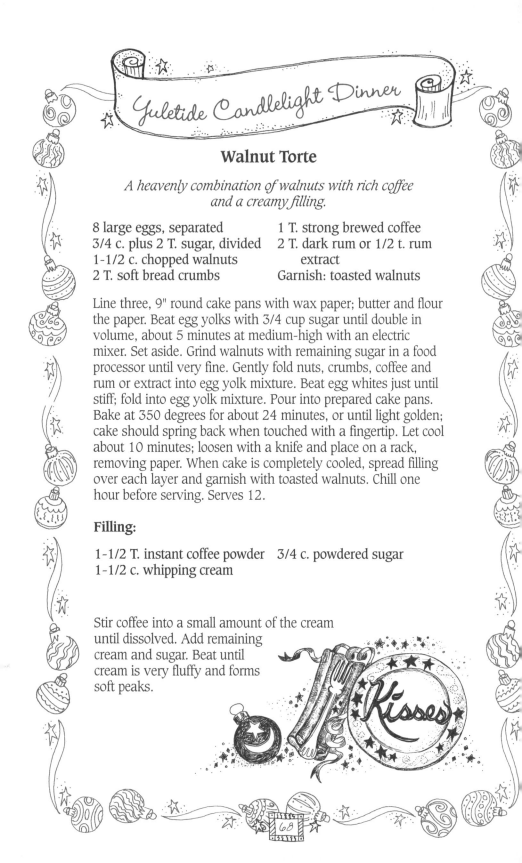

Christmas Wassail

The traditional grog for singing carols 'round the piano.

4 qts. apple cider
1 qt. orange juice
1 c. lemon juice
1 qt. pineapple juice
24 whole cloves

4 cinnamon sticks
1 c. brown sugar, packed

Mix all ingredients in a large pot and heat to almost boiling. Reduce heat and simmer about 45 minutes. Remove cinnamon and cloves before serving. Makes 1-1/2 gallons.

Old-Fashioned Eggnog

It's the real thing and there is a difference!

6 eggs
1/2 c. sugar
1/4 t. salt
3 c. milk
1 t. vanilla extract
1 t. nutmeg, divided
1 c. whipping cream

Beat eggs, sugar and salt together in a saucepan; stir in milk. Cook over medium heat, stirring, about 15 minutes or until mixture coats spoon. Remove from heat and stir in vanilla and 1/2 teaspoon nutmeg; chill overnight. Just before serving, whip cream to soft peaks; whisk into egg mixture in a gentle folding motion. Serve sprinkled with remaining nutmeg. Makes 10 servings.

Homespun Christmas Ornaments

You can make your own fabric tree ornaments so easily! Just use your favorite cookie cutters...trees, angels, Santas, gingerbread men, stars and reindeer. With a soft pencil, trace around the cutters onto the back side of a folded piece of fabric. Choose fun country fabrics like mini-checks, calicos and bright Christmas plaids. Pin the 2 sides together and cut out the shapes, then sew all around with a 1/4-inch hem, leaving an inch-wide opening for filling. Turn fabric rightside-out and fill the shape with fiberfill, cotton or sweet-smelling potpourri. Sew up the opening.

If you like, you can sew all around the outside of your ornament with colorful yarn. Add beads for eyes, sew on a smile, and add buttons and bows. This is a great project to do with the kids. They'll be so proud of their creations!

Bows for Pastries

It's so easy to make bows out of gumdrops. Just flatten a handful of large gumdrops with a rolling pin on a pastry board sprinkled with sugar. Make a large square or rectangle, then cut it into strips and form the softened gumdrops into a bow. Use it to top a Christmas cake; "wrap" the cake with ribbons to make a package!

It's an old English custom to wrap tiny treasures in paper and bake them inside the Christmas cake. A bell means a wedding soon, the thimble blesses its owner, the wishbone grants any wish and the horseshoe means good luck. Be sure to let your guests know about the surprises before they dig in!

Christmas Morning

Vanilla Coffee

A rich, mellow wake-up on Christmas day.

1-1/2 c. milk
1 T. sugar
1 t. cinnamon, divided

3 c. strong brewed coffee
1-1/2 t. vanilla extract
Garnish: whipped topping

Combine milk, sugar and 1/2 teaspoon cinnamon in a saucepan and stir well. Cook over medium heat 2 minutes, or until sugar dissolves. Remove from heat; stir in coffee and vanilla. Pour into mugs and garnish with whipped topping. Sprinkle with remaining cinnamon. Serves 4.

Fancy cream puffs so soon after breakfast. The very idea made one shudder. All the same, 2 minutes later Jose and Laura were licking their fingers with that absorbed inward look that only comes from whipped cream.
–Katherine Mansfield

Sunrise Punch

A festive brunch drink for a special occasion.

3 c. orange juice
1/2 c. plus 2 T. tequila or
    orange juice
1/4 c. lime juice

2 T. powdered sugar
2 T. orange-flavored liqueur
1 T. grenadine syrup
Garnish: lime slices

Combine all ingredients except grenadine and lime slices in a pitcher and chill. Fill 6 tall glasses with ice and pour in mixture. Slowly add 1/2 teaspoon grenadine down the inside of each glass. Garnish with lime slices. Serves 6.

Christmas Casserole

A Christmas Day favorite...make it the day before and just pop it in the oven the next morning!

5-1/2 oz. pkg. stuffing mix
1 lb. ground sausage,
    browned and drained
4 eggs
2 c. milk
10-3/4 oz. can cream of
    mushroom soup

16-oz. pkg. frozen Italian
    vegetables
1 c. Cheddar cheese, shredded
1 c. Monterey Jack cheese,
    shredded

Line the bottom of a 13"x9" baking pan with stuffing mix. Sprinkle cooked sausage over top. Beat eggs and milk until thoroughly mixed and add remaining ingredients, stirring well. Pour egg mixture over the sausage. Bake at 350 degrees for one hour. Casserole may be prepared ahead and refrigerated before baking. Serves 8.

Honey Spiced Ham

Yummy ham for sandwiches and snacking all day long.

10-lb. bone-in ham
1/2 c. whole cloves
1/2 c. honey
1/4 c. butter

1 t. cinnamon
1/2 t. ground nutmeg
1/4 t. allspice

Place ham, fat-side up, on a rack in a shallow roasting pan. Score in a diamond pattern about 1/4-inch deep. Insert cloves in center of each diamond. Bake, uncovered, at 325 degrees for about 2 hours. Combine all remaining ingredients and cook over medium heat, stirring until mixture comes to a boil. Spread glaze over ham and bake another 15 to 20 minutes. Serves 24.

Give your daughter or granddaughter a gift of some of your old costume jewelry that you no longer wear. Include an outdated, dressy dress and a cast-off pair of high heels. Put everything together in a pretty, decorated "dress up" box.

Cranberry-Orange Chutney

An excellent relish for ham sandwiches.

4 seedless oranges
1/2 c. orange juice
1 lb. cranberries
2 c. sugar
1/4 c. crystallized ginger, diced

1/2 t. hot pepper sauce
1 cinnamon stick
1 clove garlic
3/4 t. curry powder
3/4 c. golden raisins

Peel oranges, reserving the zest from 2 of them. Slice the reserved zest very thinly. Cut oranges in 1/4-inch thick slices and quarter. Combine orange zest with remaining ingredients and simmer in a saucepan over medium heat, stirring until sugar dissolves and cranberries burst. Remove from heat; discard cinnamon and garlic. Add oranges and toss lightly. Serve hot or cold with baked ham. Makes 6 cups.

Tie bright wired ribbons around your terra cotta pots to give your houseplants a holiday look!

Pumpkin Nut Bread

Easy snacking for the Christmas crowd.

3-1/4 c. all-purpose flour
3/4 c. quick oats, uncooked
2 t. baking soda
1/2 t. baking powder
1-1/2 t. pumpkin pie spice
1/2 t. salt
3 eggs

15-oz. can pumpkin
1-1/2 c. sugar
1-1/2 c. brown sugar, packed
1/2 c. water
1/2 c. vegetable oil
1/2 c. evaporated milk
1 c. walnuts, chopped

Combine flour, oats, baking soda, baking powder, spice and salt in a large bowl. Beat together eggs, pumpkin, sugars, water, oil and evaporated milk on medium speed until combined. Beat flour mixture into pumpkin mixture until blended; stir in nuts. Fill 2 greased 9"x5" loaf pans. Bake at 350 degrees for 65 to 70 minutes, or until toothpick comes out clean. Cool in pans 10 minutes; remove from pans to cool completely.
Makes 2 loaves.

Take the kids pine cone hunting…gather as many pine cones as you can find to fill baskets, then sprinkle with potpourri scents. Tie on ribbons and share them with friends and neighbors.

Keepsakes you can make...

Bay Leaf Votives

Purchase clear glass votive candleholders and white votive candles. Glue fresh glossy bay leaves around the holder with a glue gun. Tie a bow around the middle with gold florist's ribbon. This makes an extra-special place setting or favor for your guests.

Candle Cups

Shop discount department stores or thrift shops for inexpensive glasses and clear glass mugs. Look for little demitasse mugs, dessert goblets and other interesting shapes. Warm the glasses with hot water, then carefully melt wax and pour into the glasses. Add wicks. Experiment with different colors, or add dried rosebuds, straw flowers or clover blossoms to the liquid wax. These special candles make unique gifts...or scatter them about your kitchen and dining area for a warm winter glow!

Welcoming in the New Year

Smoked Salmon Canapés

For casual gatherings or fancy parties, everyone loves salmon!

1 c. sour cream
1/4 t. lemon zest
1 loaf party-size light rye
   bread, crusts removed
4 T. butter, melted

1/2 lb. smoked salmon,
   sliced and cut into
   1/4" strips
Garnish: 2 scallions, thinly
   sliced

Combine the sour cream and lemon zest and chill for 2 hours.
Brush the bread slices with butter and cut each slice in half
diagonally. Arrange bread triangles on baking sheets and bake
at 350 degrees for about 10 minutes, or until lightly toasted. Let
cool completely. Spoon chilled lemon cream on top of each toast.
Place a salmon strip on top and garnish with scallions. Makes
5 to 6 dozen.

*Toasting lore: Back in the
sixteenth century,
well-wishers used to place a
spicy crouton in the wine goblet.
The last person to drink from
the goblet claimed the "toast,"
along with good wishes for
the future.*

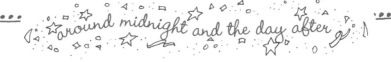
Pimento Deviled Eggs

Festive, colorful and tasty!

1 dozen large eggs,
    hard-boiled and peeled
1/4 c. pimentos, chopped
1/4 c. mayonnaise
1-1/2 t. Dijon mustard

1/2 t. paprika
1/4 t. salt
Garnish: fresh parsley and
    minced red pepper

Slice each egg lengthwise in half and remove yolks. Mash yolks
with a fork. Stir in pimentos, mayonnaise, mustard, paprika
and salt. Spoon yolk mixture into egg-white halves. (For a more
festive look, pipe the yolks into the whites with a star tip.)
Refrigerate, covered, until ready to serve. Garnish with fresh
parsley and a colorful sprinkling of red pepper. Makes 24.

*In days gone by, gentlemen would go calling at
unmarried ladies' homes on New Year's Day. The father
would greet visitors at the door (probably in his
smoking jacket), where the gentleman caller would
produce his calling card. The cards were placed in an
elaborate cut-glass bowl. Once inside, the gentlemen
enjoyed sarsaparilla and fancy tiered cakes as they
chatted politely with the young ladies.*

Patchwork Wheel of Brie

A festive centerpiece for your appetizer table.

5-lb. whole Brie cheese
1 c. currants
1 c. walnuts, finely chopped
1 c. fresh dill, chopped

1/2 c. poppy seed
1 c. blanched almonds,
   slivered
water crackers

Remove rind from the top of cheese by cutting carefully with a sharp knife. Lightly score the top of the cheese into 10 equal pie-shaped sections. Sprinkle half of each of the toppings onto each wedge and press gently until you have decorated all 10 sections. Allow to stand at room temperature for at least 40 minutes before serving. Serve with water crackers or other light wafers. Serves 20 to 25.

Long ago in Tennessee, it was the belief that, if you washed your clothes on New Year's Day, you would wash someone out of your family. And, it was considered good luck to eat black-eyed peas!

Hoppin' John

Hoppin' John is a traditional good luck stew popular in the South. Eating it on New Year's Day promises a prosperous and healthy New Year.

1 c. dried black-eyed peas
10 c. water, divided
6 slices bacon, cut up
3/4 c. onion, chopped
1 stalk celery, chopped

3/4 t. cayenne pepper
1-1/2 t. salt
1 c. long-cooking rice,
   uncooked

Rinse peas and put in large saucepan with 6 cups water. Bring to a boil; reduce heat and simmer for 2 minutes. Remove from heat, cover and let stand one hour. Drain and rinse. In same pan, cook bacon until crisp. Drain off drippings, reserving 3 tablespoons in pan. Add peas, remaining water, onion, celery, cayenne pepper and salt. Bring to a boil, cover, and reduce heat. Simmer 30 minutes. Add uncooked rice; cover and simmer 20 minutes longer, until peas and rice are tender. Serves 4 to 6.

In Louisiana, it's good luck to wear something new on New Year's Day. In North Carolina, folklore has it that rice and peas will bring you luck. You'll also have paper money all year if you eat your collard greens! In Maryland, it was tradition to have a masquerade party. All the guests would remain in masquerade until midnight, when they'd reveal their faces.

4-Cheese & Peppers Pizza

*Just double or triple this recipe if you have a
crowd of well-wishers!*

16-oz. loaf frozen bread
   dough, thawed
1 green pepper, chopped
1 red pepper, chopped
1 c. mozzarella cheese, shredded
3/4 c. fontina cheese, shredded
1/2 c. Parmesan cheese, grated

1/2 c. feta cheese, crumbled
2 cloves garlic, minced
2 t. dried parsley
3 plum tomatoes, thinly
   sliced
1 T. olive oil

Press bread dough into a greased 12" pizza pan. Prick
generously with a fork. Bake in a 375-degree oven for 20 to
25 minutes, until light brown. Top with peppers, cheeses, garlic,
parsley and tomatoes; brush olive oil over the top. Bake in
375-degree oven for 15 to 20 minutes, or until cheese is
melted. Let stand for a few minutes before cutting. Serves 6.

*Use tiny pretzel sticks
instead of toothpicks for
spearing cheese cubes.*

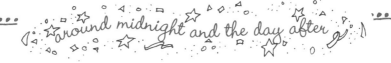

Overnight Pork & Sauerkraut

*Traditionally, eating pork and sauerkraut on New Year's Day
will bring you good luck. Put this casserole in the oven in the
wee small hours of the morning, and it'll be ready
for you on New Year's Day!*

2 lbs. pork loin, cut
    into 1" cubes
2 lbs. sauerkraut

2 c. onion, sliced
6 slices bacon, cut in half
3 c. water

Brown pork in a large skillet and set aside. Place one pound of
sauerkraut in a 2-quart casserole dish. Cover with one cup
onion and the pork. Top with remaining onion and sauerkraut.
Top with bacon. Pour water over the layers and bake,
uncovered, at 300 degrees overnight, or about 7 to 8 hours.
Serves 4 to 6.

Apple Kugel

A very soothing noodle "pudding"!

8-oz. pkg. medium egg,
    noodles, uncooked
4 T. vegetable oil, divided
4 large eggs
1/3 c. sugar
1 c. orange juice

1/4 t. cinnamon
1/8 t. ground ginger
1/8 t. salt
1 large apple, cored, peeled
    and diced

Cook noodles according to package directions; drain and toss with
2 tablespoons oil. In a large bowl, mix eggs, sugar, orange juice,
seasonings and remaining oil. Add apples. Combine mixture with
noodles and transfer to a greased 10"x10" casserole dish. Cover
and bake at 350 degrees for 40 minutes. Uncover and bake an
additional 10 to 20 minutes. Cut into squares. Makes 12 servings.

*A bit of German folklore…if you keep
herring or cabbage in the house on New Year's Eve,
you'll have money all year. If you eat a piece of
herring as the clock strikes midnight, you'll be
lucky all year.*

Monte Cristos

*A hearty breakfast sandwich for those
after-midnight munchies.*

1/2 c. butter, divided
8 thin slices bread, crusts
    removed
4 large thin slices ham

4 slices sweet onion
1/2 lb. Cheddar cheese, grated
4 eggs
salt and pepper to taste

On a large griddle, melt half the butter and fry 4 slices of bread on one side until brown. Remove from griddle and place slices uncooked sides down. Place a slice of ham, a slice of onion and 1/2 cup cheese on each piece of bread. Place the other slice of bread on top of each stack, with the browned side down. Beat eggs with a little salt and pepper; coat outsides of sandwiches with eggs. Melt remaining butter on the griddle; fry sandwiches on each side until golden. Slice each in half diagonally; serve immediately. Makes 4 servings.

Early American folklore says that the lady of the house would open first the front door, and then the back door, letting the cold air flow through the house. After a moment she would say, "letting out the old and letting in the new!"

Potato Rivel Soup

A cup of this hearty Pennsylvania Dutch soup will warm the coldest New Year!

5 potatoes, diced	4 to 6 c. milk
1 medium onion, chopped	1/2 c. butter
2 eggs, beaten	1/8 t. celery seed
1/2 c. all-purpose flour	salt and pepper to taste
1 t. salt	Garnish: fresh parsley

Cover potatoes and onion with water; boil until potatoes are soft. Beat eggs in a bowl; add flour and salt to eggs and stir until mixture is lumpy. Drop bits of egg mixture (the "rivels") into the potato mixture and simmer for 10 to 15 minutes. Add milk, butter and celery seed; heat through. Add salt and pepper to taste; garnish with parsley. Serves 6.

Laugh and be merry together, like brothers akin,
Guesting awhile in the room of a beautiful inn.
Glad till the dancing stops, and the lilt of
the music ends.
Laugh till the game is played;
and be you merry my friends.
-John Masefield

Rich Rum Cake

*There can be no holiday without a delicious rum cake! Garnish
with fresh orange slices or chopped nuts.*

4 eggs, separated
1/2 c. brown sugar, packed
   and divided
1 c. all-purpose flour

1 t. baking powder
1/4 t. salt
1/3 c. butter, melted
1 t. vanilla extract

Beat egg whites until stiff; add 4 tablespoons brown sugar. Beat
yolks with remaining sugar; add to egg white mixture. Fold in
flour, baking powder and salt; add butter and vanilla. Pour into
a greased and floured tube pan; bake at 375 degrees for 25 to
30 minutes. Remove from oven; poke holes in the top with a
long skewer. Drizzle rum sauce over cake. Serves 10 to 12.

Rum Sauce:

1/4 c. butter
1 c. orange juice

1/2 c. powdered sugar
1/2 c. rum

Melt butter in a small saucepan. Add orange juice and sugar; stir
until sugar is dissolved. Add rum and heat through.

*Life begets life. Energy creates
energy. It is by spending oneself
that one becomes rich.*
-Sarah Bernhardt

Your own special way...

Ornament Centerpiece

Fill a large, round glass bowl such as a salad bowl, punch bowl or trifle bowl, heaping full of shiny, bright gold and silver ornaments. Wind little white fairy lights around and through the arrangement. Use clear glass plates and gold napkins to complete a festive look for your table. Reflects candlelight and makes a glowing centerpiece...perfect for New Year's Eve!

Christmas Tree Bird Feeder

When you're finished with your tree, prop it up outside and decorate it with food for the birds. Fill the crevices of pine cones with peanut butter, and fill grapefruit or orange rinds with birdseed. Tie to the branches with string. The birds will "decorate" your tree before you know it!

If you've strung your Christmas tree with popcorn, be sure to hang the garland outside for the birds after the tree comes down! (Make sure the garland has no leftover hooks or tinsel hanging around.)

Chocolate Mousse

Silky, smooth and creamy.

6-oz. pkg. semi-sweet
   chocolate chips
2 T. sugar
1/2 c. butter

3/4 c. whipping cream
3 pasteurized eggs, separated
1/2 t. vanilla extract

In a double boiler, melt chocolate with butter over simmering water. Pour into a bowl and allow to cool to room temperature. Add egg yolks to chocolate and stir well. In a separate mixing bowl, beat egg whites to soft peaks; add sugar while beating. Whisk a little bit of the egg white into the chocolate mixture, then gently fold in the rest. Whip cream and vanilla together until stiff; gently fold into chocolate mixture. Spoon into serving dishes and chill. Serves 4.

Spread melted chocolate generously on one side of a sugar cookie. Press another cookie on top to make a sandwich. You can melt the chocolate squares or chips in the microwave or a double boiler. Put your sandwich cookies in the fridge to set for a few minutes... then decorate!

Chocolate Orange Cake

Citrusy flavor combines with chocolate for an irresistible treat!

1/2 c. plus 2 T. butter, divided
1 c. sugar
4 eggs, separated
1 c. all-purpose flour
12-oz. pkg. semi-sweet chocolate chips, melted
6 T. orange liqueur, divided
2 c. powdered sugar
1/3 c. white chocolate chips, melted
3 T. orange juice
Garnish: orange slices, chocolate curls

Grease and flour a 9" springform pan. Beat together 1/2 cup butter and sugar on high setting of mixer. Add egg yolks. Beat in flour and stir in melted chocolate. Add 4 tablespoons liqueur. Beat egg whites until stiff. Stir one cup of the whites into flour mixture; then fold in remaining whites. Spread batter into the pan and bake at 350 degrees for 45 minutes, or until done when tested with a toothpick. Cool at least 15 minutes, then remove cake from pan. To make frosting, combine powdered sugar, melted white chocolate, orange juice and remaining liqueur. Spread over cake. Chill and garnish with orange slices and grated chocolate curls. Serves 6 to 8.

Chocolate curls are elegant for garnishing cakes, desserts or hot chocolate. Here's how: Soften white or semi-sweet chocolate by microwaving repeatedly for 8 seconds, or until soft. Use a sharp vegetable peeler and, peeling toward you, make the curls. Or, melt chocolate into a flat baking pan and use a small, flat metal spatula to scrape up large curls.

Frosty Chocolate-Pecan Pie

This frozen concoction is delightfully rich and crunchy.

Crust:

2 c. pecans, finely chopped
    and toasted
5 T. brown sugar, packed
5 T. butter, diced

Optional: 2 t. dark rum
1/2 c. whipping cream
Garnish: semi-sweet
    chocolate shavings

Blend nuts, sugar, butter and rum, if using. Press into bottom and sides of a 9" pie plate. Freeze for one hour. Pour filling into prepared crust, cover and freeze. One hour before serving, transfer pie to refrigerator. Whip cream and pipe on top of pie filling. Garnish with chocolate shavings. Serves 6 to 8.

Filling:

6-oz. pkg. semi-sweet
    chocolate chips
1/2 t. instant coffee powder
4 eggs, room temperature

Optional: 1 T. dark rum
1 t. vanilla extract
1 c. whipping cream

Melt chocolate with coffee in the top of a double boiler over hot water. Remove from heat and whisk in eggs, rum (if using) and vanilla until mixture is smooth. Allow to cool about 5 minutes. Whip cream until stiff. Gently fold whipped cream into chocolate mixture until blended completely.

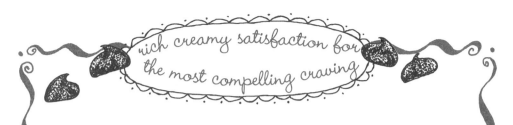

Sweet Chocolate Chunk Cookies

America's favorite cookie, now with big, chewy chunks.

3 c. all-purpose flour
1-1/2 t. baking soda
1-1/2 t. salt
1-1/2 c. butter
1-1/2 c. sugar
3/4 c. brown sugar, packed

3 eggs
1 T. vanilla extract
12 oz. sweet baking
   chocolate, chopped into
   chunks
1-1/2 c. walnuts, chopped

Mix flour, soda and salt. In a separate bowl, cream butter; beat in sugars, eggs and vanilla until light and fluffy. Blend in flour mixture. Add chocolate and nuts; chill for about an hour. For each cookie, measure 1/4 cup dough on an ungreased baking sheet and flatten slightly. Bake 4 to 5 at a time on one sheet at 375 degrees for 12 to 14 minutes, or until lightly browned. Cool a minute or 2 before removing from sheet. Makes 36 big cookies.

Chocolate Cookie Balls

Try creating these elegant chocolate confections with a white chocolate topping, too.

2 large egg whites
1 c. sugar
2 T. unsweetened baking
   cocoa

1-1/2 c. toasted almonds,
   ground medium-fine
2/3 c. semi-sweet chocolate
   chips, melted

Beat egg whites until stiff on high speed of an electric mixer. Add sugar and continue beating until egg whites are very thick, 2 to 3 minutes. Beat in cocoa; stir in almonds and blend completely. Line a baking sheet with waxed paper. With damp hands, shape heaping teaspoonfuls of dough into one-inch balls. Place on baking sheet about 2 inches apart. Bake at 325 degrees about 15 minutes, or until cookies begin to crack slightly. Allow to cool 10 minutes; transfer to a rack. Dip the top of each cooled cookie into melted chocolate and allow to harden. Makes 2 dozen.

Chocolate Bavarian Cream

Rich, smooth and satisfying.

1 env. unflavored gelatin
1/4 c. cold water
dash of salt
1/2 c. sugar
1 c. milk

2 sqs. unsweetened
   chocolate, melted
1 c. whipping cream
1 t. vanilla extract

Soften gelatin in water; set aside. Mix egg yolks, salt and sugar over hot water in the top of a double boiler. Blend in milk over hot water gradually, cooking and stirring constantly until over hot water mixture is thick and smooth. Stir in melted chocolate. Add gelatin; stir until dissolved. Cool. Whip cream; add vanilla and fold into cooled mixture. Spoon into a one-quart mold and chill. Serves 4.

White Chocolate Mousse Pastries

Ready-made pastry shells are the secret to this easy, elegant dessert!

10-oz. pkg. frozen puff
   pastry shells
6 sqs. white chocolate
1-1/2 c. whipping cream,
   divided

1 sq. semi-sweet
   chocolate, melted

Follow baking directions on pastry shell package; let shells cool. Place white chocolate and 1/4 cup whipping cream in a microwave container; heat 2 minutes on high, until chocolate is almost melted. Stir until completely melted. Cool until chocolate reaches room temperature, stirring occasionally. Beat remaining cream in a chilled bowl with electric mixer until soft peaks form. Fold half of the whipped cream into the white chocolate, then fold in the other half just until blended. Spoon into the pastry shells. Drizzle melted semi-sweet chocolate over the top. Chill overnight. Serves 6.

White Chocolate Chip-Macadamia Nut Brownie Pie

The crunchy macadamia nuts combine with the creamy white chocolate to create a fabulous taste sensation.

1/2 c. butter, softened
1 c. sugar
2 eggs
1/2 c. all-purpose flour
1/4 c. unsweetened baking
  cocoa

1 t. vanilla extract
1/2 c. macadamia nuts,
  chopped
1/2 c. white chocolate chips
vanilla ice cream

Cream butter and sugar together and beat in eggs. Add flour, cocoa and vanilla. Fold in nuts and chips. Pour into a greased 9" pie pan. Bake at 325 degrees for 35 minutes. Pie should be moist; toothpick will not come out completely clean. Let cool slightly; serve with a scoop of vanilla ice cream on the side. Serves 6 to 8.

I don't think a really good pie can be made without a dozen or so children peeking over your shoulder as you stoop to look in at it every little while.
-John Gould

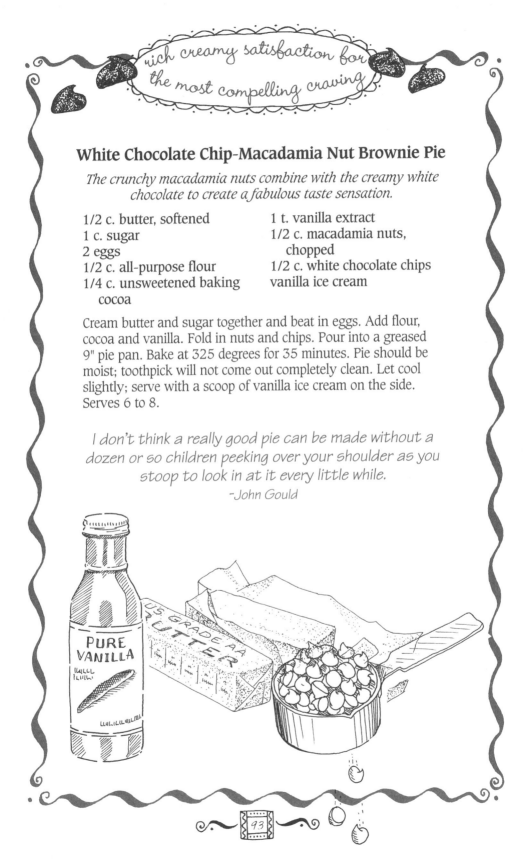

Crème de Menthe Sheet Cake

This cool mint cake makes an excellent holiday dessert.

1 c. sugar
1/2 c. butter, softened
4 eggs
1 c. all-purpose flour

12-oz. can chocolate syrup
Garnish: crushed pepper-
    mints, chocolate sprinkles

Beat together sugar and butter; add eggs, flour and syrup.
Pour into a greased and floured 13"x9" baking pan; bake at
350 degrees for 25 to 30 minutes. Let cool; frost. Sprinkle with
crushed peppermints or chocolate sprinkles. Serves 12 to 15.

Frosting:

2-1/2 c. powdered sugar
1/2 c. butter, softened
6 T. crème de menthe
    liqueur

12-oz. pkg. semi-sweet
    chocolate chips, melted
1 to 2 T. milk

Combine all ingredients, adjusting milk for desired consistency.
Beat with an electric mixer until smooth.

Hot Fudge Sauce

Keep an extra jar in the fridge for late-night snacks!

1/2 c. unsweetened
    baking cocoa
1 c. sour cream

1-1/2 c. sugar
1 t. vanilla extract
vanilla or coffee ice cream

In a double boiler, stir all ingredients together. Cook for one
hour over low heat, stirring occasionally. Drizzle over vanilla or
coffee ice cream. Makes one pint.

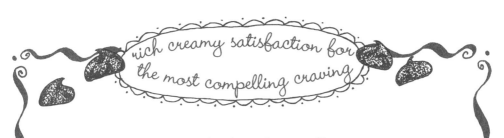

French Chocolate Balls

So rich, so chocolatey, crunchy on the outside and soft on the inside...a chocolate lover's dream!

2 eggs
1/2 c. plus 3 T. sugar
4 sqs. unsweetened baking
   chocolate, grated
1/2 t. cinnamon
1 t. vanilla extract

5 T. plus 1 t. all-purpose
   flour
2 c. plus 6 T. almonds,
   finely ground
1 c. powdered sugar

Beat eggs together with sugar until light and fluffy. Add remaining ingredients; beat well. Pat dough into a ball and chill for one hour. Spoon out dough and shape into one-inch balls; roll balls in powdered sugar. Allow to dry for several hours on a greased baking sheet. Bake at 475 degrees for 4 minutes, or until a light crust forms on balls. Allow to cool for 10 minutes on the baking sheet; remove to cooling rack. Makes about 4 dozen.

Aren't you clever...

Chocolate Cake Topper

To make a chocolate disk cake topper, melt white or milk chocolate over a double boiler and stir until smooth. Pour chocolate out onto a wax paper-lined baking sheet. Allow chocolate to set slightly, then invert a small bowl on top of it. Using the bowl as a guide, cut around the edge of the bowl with an icing spreader and you'll have a perfect circle. Freeze. Remove chocolate disk from the freezer and, using an icing tip or a plastic bag with a tiny corner cut off, pipe on your greeting with melted white or dark chocolate. Freeze until set. Place disk in the center of iced cake and serve.

Chocolate Garnishes

Garnish sheet cakes with chocolate cut-outs or fancy chocolate leaves. It's easier than you think! To make the cut-outs, pour melted milk chocolate onto a wax paper-lined baking sheet. Allow chocolate to set slightly at room temperature. Using your favorite mini cookie cutter shapes, cut out the chocolate and remove with a thin metal spatula, placing them again on the wax paper-lined sheet. Freeze until firm. To create chocolate leaves, paint the vein side of a non-toxic leaf with melted chocolate. Place in the refrigerator until set; gently peel off the leaf.

Different types of chocolate and their uses

Melting chocolate - Perfect for dipping strawberries and making your own homemade candies. For a real chocolate fix (or quick, thoughtful gift) dip double-cream chocolate sandwich cookies (store-bought) into melted milk or dark chocolate. Let set, then drizzle with melted white chocolate.

Semi-sweet chocolate - Pure chocolate perfection. Available in chunks or chips, semi-sweet chocolate has less sugar content and is just right for making chocolate chip cookies or muffins.

Dark chocolate - Pure chocolate with a smooth, rich flavor, not quite as sweet as milk chocolate. Use either dark or milk chocolate in candy-making and baking, depending on your personal preference.

Milk chocolate - Pure chocolate mixed with extra cocoa butter and sugar. Sweet, smooth and a favorite for snackers.

Cocoa powder - Use for baking cakes, brownies, making frostings and hot chocolate. Extra bonus: cocoa powder is naturally low in fat and cholesterol-free. A good low-fat alternative to baking with chocolate is to replace each square of baking chocolate with 3 level tablespoons of cocoa plus one tablespoon of vegetable oil. For an extra-special treat, try sprinkling sweetened cocoa powder on top of vanilla ice cream or yogurt. Yum!

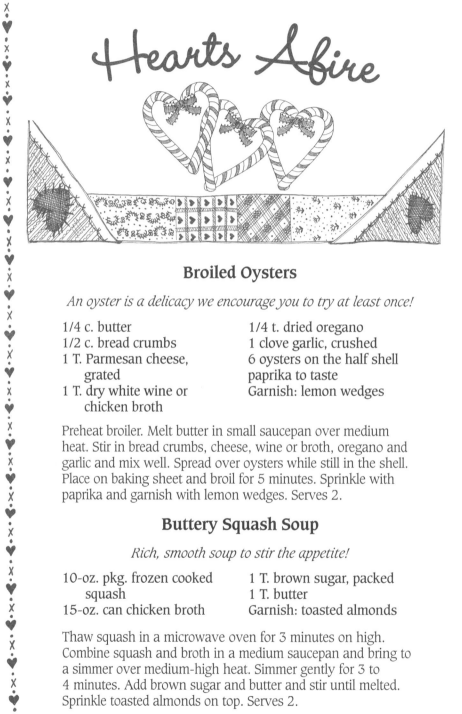

Hearts Afire

Broiled Oysters

An oyster is a delicacy we encourage you to try at least once!

1/4 c. butter
1/2 c. bread crumbs
1 T. Parmesan cheese, grated
1 T. dry white wine or chicken broth

1/4 t. dried oregano
1 clove garlic, crushed
6 oysters on the half shell
paprika to taste
Garnish: lemon wedges

Preheat broiler. Melt butter in small saucepan over medium heat. Stir in bread crumbs, cheese, wine or broth, oregano and garlic and mix well. Spread over oysters while still in the shell. Place on baking sheet and broil for 5 minutes. Sprinkle with paprika and garnish with lemon wedges. Serves 2.

Buttery Squash Soup

Rich, smooth soup to stir the appetite!

10-oz. pkg. frozen cooked squash
15-oz. can chicken broth

1 T. brown sugar, packed
1 T. butter
Garnish: toasted almonds

Thaw squash in a microwave oven for 3 minutes on high. Combine squash and broth in a medium saucepan and bring to a simmer over medium-high heat. Simmer gently for 3 to 4 minutes. Add brown sugar and butter and stir until melted. Sprinkle toasted almonds on top. Serves 2.

Tempting Caesar Salad

A crisp, green classic.

2 anchovy fillets
2/3 c. olive oil
3 T. lemon juice
1 t. white wine vinegar
1/4 t. salt
1/2 t. pepper

1 pasteurized egg
1/2 large head romaine
  lettuce, torn
1/3 c. Parmesan cheese,
  grated

Mash anchovies in a wooden bowl. Add olive oil, lemon juice, vinegar, salt and pepper; mix well. Whisk in egg. Add lettuce and toss well. Sprinkle with Parmesan cheese and Garlic Croutons. Serves 2.

Garlic Croutons:

3 T. olive oil
1 clove garlic, crushed

1 c. day-old French bread,
  cubed

Heat oil and garlic in a skillet. Add bread cubes; toss over low heat until golden.

Seen on a fortune cookie: The first person you see on Valentine's Day will be your valentine.

Roast Cornish Hens

Plump, tender hens, one for each of you, are easy, fun and delicious.

2 1-lb. Rock Cornish hens	salt and pepper to taste
2 T. vegetable oil	garlic powder to taste

Rub hens with oil and season inside and out; place in an uncovered roasting pan. Roast at 375 degrees for approximately one hour, or until juices run clear when pierced and a meat thermometer registers 180 degrees at inner thigh. Serves 2.

Make a love note jar for your family. Use a big, wide-mouthed pickle jar, and have each family member tuck one or 2 love notes into the jar about a week before Valentine's Day. (Don't forget to decorate the jar with ribbons, hearts and cupids!) On Valentine's Day, each person gets to draw a love note. The notes can vary from coupons to wash dishes and do laundry, to simple messages telling family members why you love them.

Filet Mignons Flambé

Tempt your love with the tenderest cut of beef, marinated and seared to juicy perfection.

2 6-oz. filet mignon steaks	1/2 T. vegetable oil
1/4 c. cognac, divided	2 large shallots, minced
1/2 t. coarse pepper	1/4 c. beef broth
1 T. butter, divided	salt to taste

Sprinkle meat with one tablespoon cognac; let stand at room temperature for 45 minutes. Rub meat with the pepper. In a heavy skillet, melt 1/2 tablespoon butter in the oil. When the skillet is hot enough that a drop of water bounces off the surface, add meat. Cover partially; cook over high heat about 2 minutes, or until bottom is seared. Turn and cook another 2 minutes on the other side. Reduce heat to medium; continue cooking about 2 minutes longer per side. Transfer meat to a warm plate. Melt remaining butter in the skillet with the oil; add the shallots and cook over medium-high heat until shallots are translucent. Add remaining cognac to the skillet and ignite with a match. Cook over high until the flame extinguishes itself, about 30 seconds. Add the beef broth, stir, and boil until liquid is reduced to 1/4 cup. Spoon sauce over the meat and sprinkle with salt to taste. Serves 2.

Find anything and everything heart-shaped that you own and create a Valentine's Day centerpiece. Use heart-shaped cookie cutters, pillows, sachets, or construction paper hearts. String red and pink ribbons throughout for a fun table setting.

Roasted Baby Red Potatoes

Crispy and golden...perfect with roasted meats!

6 new red potatoes
2 T. olive oil
salt and pepper to taste

2 cloves garlic, minced
1 T. fresh Italian parsley,
   chopped

Prick potatoes with a fork and arrange on a baking sheet. Bake at 350 degrees for 1-1/2 hours. Cut into quarters; place in a warm bowl and toss with remaining ingredients. Serves 2 to 4.

Chocolate Puffs

Puff pastry makes it so easy to do!

1 sheet frozen puff pastry
6-oz. pkg. semi-sweet
   chocolate chips

1/4 c. walnuts, chopped
Garnish: powdered sugar

Let pastry thaw for 30 minutes. Roll out on a lightly floured surface to a 12-inch square. Cut into four, 6-inch squares. In the center of each, spoon 1/4 cup chips and one tablespoon nuts. Bring up all 4 corners of each square, join the corners and twist. Fan out corners. Bake on an ungreased baking sheet at 425 degrees for 10 to 15 minutes, or until golden. Let stand 10 minutes; sprinkle with powdered sugar. Makes 4 servings.

Another simple, easy dessert... make or buy a dreamy, white angel food cake. Make it extra luscious with strawberry whipped cream filling, or drizzle with fresh raspberry sauce. Sprinkle with candy confetti or red hots for added sizzle.

Handmade from the heart...

Heart Centerpiece

heart-shaped box   one bag cranberries
florist foam   toothpicks
tacky glue   raffia
Spanish moss

Nest the bottom of the box inside the lid so the lid will serve as the base. Cut a piece of florist foam to fill the bottom of the box. Cover the foam with tacky glue and glue on the Spanish moss. Pierce cranberries individually with toothpicks so that the tip of toothpick is embedded in the berry. (A great job for the kids!) Stick the berries into the moss and continue until the top is completely covered. Tie raffia or a fabric ribbon around the outside edges of the box, finishing with a big bow at the top of the heart.

Drizzle a loving message on dessert plates with chocolate syrup.

Handmade Frame

Give your sweetie a new photo of yourself in a special frame. Purchase an unfinished wood frame and handpaint it with glittery hearts using gold and silver metallic acrylic paints. You can add a sparkly French-wire ribbon attached with a glue gun. Or découpage vintage valentine cut-outs or stickers onto the frame by arranging cut-outs and brushing with several coats of découpage medium. Your valentine will love it!

Sweetheart Cookies

Make your favorite sugar cookie recipe; cut into heart shapes. Sprinkle with pink sugar crystals. Melt a handful of chocolate chips, or a solid chocolate candy bar, in a plastic zipping bag in the microwave. Snip off a tiny corner of the bag and make squiggly designs or write special secret messages to your loved ones. Put a cookie or 2 at each place setting.

Luck O' the Irish

New England Boiled Dinner

Traditional Irish fare from colonial days.

4-lb. corned beef brisket
6 to 8 carrots, peeled
8 medium potatoes,
    peeled
6 to 8 small parsnips, peeled

1 head cabbage, cut into
    eighths
salt and pepper to taste
fresh parsley, chopped

In a large soup pot, cover beef brisket with water. Bring to a
rolling boil for 5 minutes, skimming the froth that comes to the
surface. Reduce heat to very low and simmer, covered, 3 to
4 hours until meat is tender. Add the vegetables to the water,
cooking until tender. Season with salt and pepper. Arrange sliced
meat and vegetables on a large platter, sprinkled with fresh
chopped parsley. Serves 6 to 8.

For each petal on the shamrock
This brings a wish your way:
Good health, good luck, and happiness
For today and every day.
      -Irish toast

Colcannon

The original Irish "comfort food."

1 lb. kale or cabbage, shredded	6 scallions, finely chopped
pinch of salt	2/3 c. milk or half-and-half
1 lb. potatoes	pepper to taste
	4 to 6 T. butter, melted

Cook the kale or cabbage in boiling salted water until very tender, 10 to 20 minutes. Drain well and set aside. Cook the potatoes until tender, then drain and peel them. Return to heat and mash until very smooth; set aside. In a small saucepan, combine scallions and milk and simmer for about 5 minutes. Gradually add this liquid to the potatoes, beating until fluffy. Mix in the cabbage and pepper. Heat through. Transfer to individual dishes, making a well in the center for melted butter. Serves 4 to 6.

Did you ever eat colcannon
that's made from thickened cream,
with greens and scallions blended
like a picture in your dream?
Did you ever take potato cake
when you went off to school
tucked beneath your jacket
with your book and slate and rule?
–Irish children's rhyme

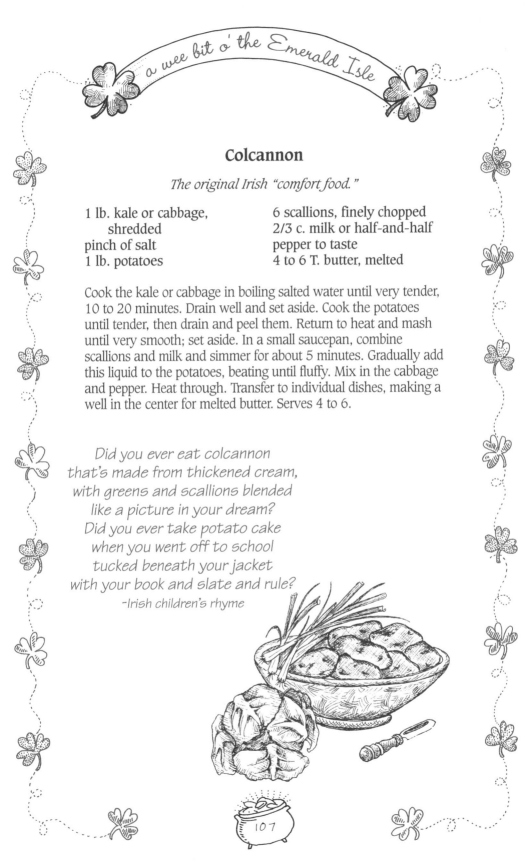

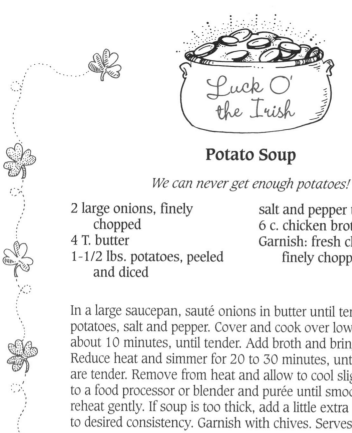

Luck O' the Irish

Potato Soup

We can never get enough potatoes!

2 large onions, finely
  chopped
4 T. butter
1-1/2 lbs. potatoes, peeled
  and diced

salt and pepper to taste
6 c. chicken broth
Garnish: fresh chives,
  finely chopped

In a large saucepan, sauté onions in butter until tender. Add potatoes, salt and pepper. Cover and cook over low heat for about 10 minutes, until tender. Add broth and bring to a boil. Reduce heat and simmer for 20 to 30 minutes, until vegetables are tender. Remove from heat and allow to cool slightly. Transfer to a food processor or blender and purée until smooth. To serve, reheat gently. If soup is too thick, add a little extra broth or milk to desired consistency. Garnish with chives. Serves 6 to 8.

Irish Soda Bread

*Serve with sweet butter, or try our herb butter blend
recipe at the end of this chapter!*

4 c. all-purpose flour	1 t. baking soda
1/2 t. salt	1 c. buttermilk

Preheat oven to 425 degrees. In mixing bowl, combine flour,
salt and soda. Stir in buttermilk and mix to a soft dough
consistency. Turn onto a floured work surface and knead lightly.
Press out into a flat, round cake, about 2 inches high. Slice an
"X" in the top. Place on a floured baking sheet and bake for
30 to 40 minutes or until lightly browned. When done, it will
sound hollow when tapped. Cool on wire rack. Makes one loaf.

*May the roof above us never fall in,
and may we friends gathered here never fall out.*
-Irish blessing

Luck O'
the Irish

Spinach-Onion Casserole

A quick, easy company casserole.

1-1/4 lbs. spinach
1 pkg. onion soup mix
1 pt. sour cream

Optional: 2 T. sherry
1 small can French fried
   onion rings

Cook the spinach in a small amount of boiling salted water until limp. Drain and press out excess water. Combine spinach, soup mix, sour cream and sherry, if using; spoon the mixture into a casserole dish. Sprinkle with onion rings and bake at 350 degrees about 20 minutes, or until bubbling hot. Serves 4.

Faith, I wish I were a leprechaun
Beneath a hawthorn tree,
A-cobblin' wee, magic boots,
A-eatin' luscious, lovely fruits;
Oh fiddle-dum, oh fiddle-dee,
I wish I were a leprechaun
Beneath a hawthorn tree!
-Margaret Ritter

Raspberry Crumble

Top with freshly whipped cream.

1 lb. raspberries
6 to 8 T. sugar
1/2 c. butter

1-2/3 c. whole wheat flour
2/3 c. rolled oats, uncooked
1/2 c. brown sugar, packed

Preheat oven to 350 degrees. Line bottom of a 9" pie plate with raspberries; sprinkle sugar over them. In a mixing bowl, cut butter into flour and blend with pastry blender until crumbly. Stir in oats and brown sugar and mix well; sprinkle on top of berries. Bake for 40 to 45 minutes until the top is golden. Serves 6.

Luck O' the Irish

Fruit Meringue Chantilly

Fancy meringues were very popular in the olden days, and remain a New England treat!

1-1/2 c. egg whites, room temperature
3/4 t. cream of tartar
pinch of salt
2-1/4 c. sugar
3 navel oranges, peeled and sectioned
1 banana, sliced and brushed with lemon juice

1 pineapple, peeled and cored
3/4 c. seedless green grapes
1/2 c. seedless purple grapes
1 kiwi fruit, peeled and sliced
3 c. whipping cream
3/4 c. powdered sugar
2 t. vanilla extract
Garnish: additional fruit, sweet chocolate, grated

Beat egg whites with cream of tartar and salt at high speed until stiff peaks are formed. Gradually beat in sugar, checking to be sure meringue is still stiff with each addition of sugar. Drop spoonfuls of meringue onto 2 greased and floured baking sheets, about 1-1/4 inches apart. Bake in a preheated, 275-degree oven for one hour, until crisp. Cool on a wire rack. While meringues are baking, cut fruit into bite-sized pieces. Whip the heavy cream with the powdered sugar and vanilla. Fold fruit into the whipped cream. On a pretty platter, layer some of the meringues in a circle. Using the fruit and cream to stick the meringues together, continue layering the meringues to form a tree-shaped dessert. Garnish with fruit and sprinkle with chocolate. Serves 10.

Plant a fruit tree... apple, peach, pear or plum. It will give you blossoms in springtime, shade in summer, luscious fruits in fall, and fragrant branches for firewood in winter.

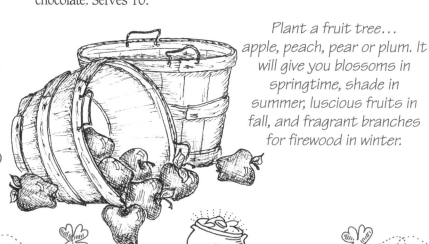

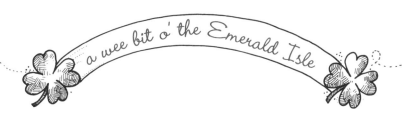

Iced Shamrock Cookies

A little fun on St. Patty's Day!

2 c. shortening
2-1/2 c. sugar
1-1/2 t. orange zest
1-1/2 t. vanilla extract
3 eggs

1/4 c. orange juice
6 c. all-purpose flour
1-1/2 t. baking powder
3/4 t. salt

Cream together shortening, sugar, orange zest and vanilla. Add eggs; mix well. Add orange juice; mix again. Sift flour, baking powder and salt together; add to creamed mixture. Chill for 2 hours, covered. Roll out 1/4-inch thick on lightly floured surface. Cut out 3 heart shapes for each shamrock and carefully press them together. Cut out a rectangle for the "stem." Bake at 375 degrees for 7 to 10 minutes. Cool completely before removing from baking sheets; frost. Makes about 6 dozen.

Frosting:

1 c. powdered sugar
2 T. butter, softened
2 to 3 T. milk, divided

peppermint extract to taste
green food coloring
Optional: crystallized sugar

Combine sugar, butter and 2 tablespoons milk in a bowl and mix. Add extract and coloring as desired. Add more milk, one teaspoon at a time, until frosting is smooth and spreadable. Sprinkle with fairy dust (crystallized sugar) if desired.

Life is like a cup of tea,
it's all in how you make it.
-Irish proverb

Luck O'
the Irish

Herb Butter Blend

*Try this on your Irish soda bread! For best results, use
freshly-dried herbs from the garden.*

1 T. dried chives
1 T. dried basil
1 T. dried parsley
1 T. dried rosemary

1 T. dried marjoram
1 T. dried tarragon
1 t. garlic powder

Mix all ingredients, using a mortar and pestle or small coffee
grinder to crush the herbs for best flavor. Store in an airtight jar.
To use, combine one tablespoon of herb blend mixture with
1/2 pound softened butter or cream cheese, mixing well. For
extra flavor, add 2 to 3 drops of lemon juice as well. Delicious
on freshly baked bread or over fresh steamed vegetables.
Makes about 1/3 cup of herb blend mixture.

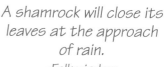

*A shamrock will close its
leaves at the approach
of rain.*
-Folk wisdom

Herbal Housekeeping

Herbal recipes for housekeeping have been handed down for generations, and you can still use them today. Herbs are economical and earth-friendly. Here are just a few natural remedies.

Herbal Vinegar Cleaner:
Fill a canning jar 3/4 full with white vinegar and add some herbs such as basil or lemon verbena from your garden. Let it stand in a sunny spot for a few days and then strain. Use herbal vinegar from a spray bottle to clean your oven and make windows sparkle. For windows, dilute a few tablespoons of vinegar in a quart of water. Use newspapers instead of paper towels to polish windows.

Lemon Balm Polish:
Simply wrap lemon balm leaves in a square of cheesecloth to polish wood furniture. The oil also acts to keep cats away from furniture.

Cinnamon Air Freshener:
A quick and easy cinnamon recipe will erase stale cooking odors. Simply stir a few teaspoons of ground cinnamon into 2 cups of hot water and let simmer for awhile on the stove.

"Soap" for Fine Washables:
Use soapwort leaves, crushed and mixed with hot water and then strained, to make a gentle fabric wash. Especially nice for silk fabrics.

Tansy Pest Repellent:
Repel flies, fleas and ants with little muslin bags filled with tansy leaves. To keep mosquitoes away, use leaves of pennyroyal. And to repel moths, make bags of lavender, basil, rosemary or peppermint leaves. Hang the bags in your closets.

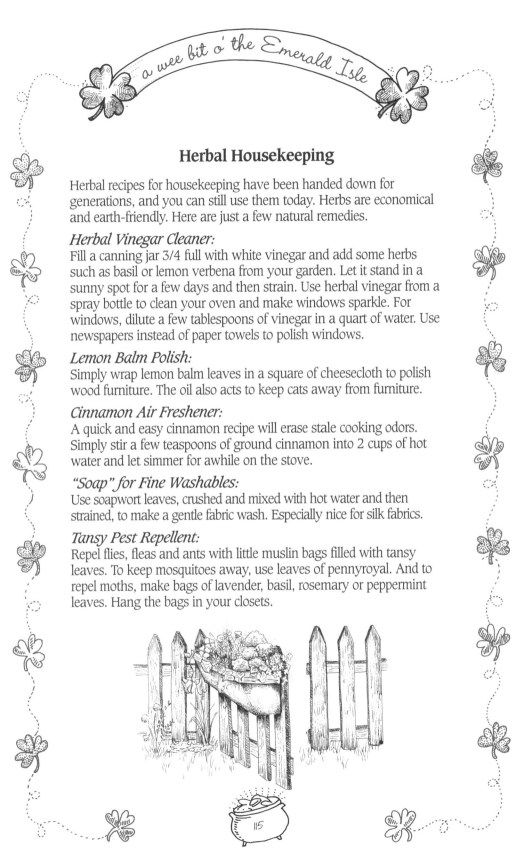

Spring Buffet

Mushroom Turnovers

A favorite appetizer...delicious with soup!

8-oz. pkg. cream cheese, softened
1/2 c. butter, softened
1-1/2 c. all-purpose flour
1 egg white, beaten

Blend cream cheese and butter until smooth. Stir in flour with a pastry blender until blended and doughy. Form into 2 balls. Wrap in plastic; refrigerate for one hour. Roll out chilled dough very thin; cut out circles with a 2-3/4" round cookie cutter. Fill each circle with a heaping teaspoon of mushroom filling; fold dough over filling and seal edges with a fork. Brush tops with beaten egg white and place on ungreased baking sheets. Bake at 400 degrees until golden, 10 to 12 minutes. Serve warm. Makes about 4 dozen.

Mushroom Filling:

1/2 lb. mushrooms, finely chopped
1 small onion, finely chopped
2 cloves garlic, finely chopped
1 T. dried thyme
2 T. butter
2 T. all-purpose flour
3 T. sour cream
1 T. soy sauce
1/2 t. salt

In a large skillet over medium heat, sauté mushrooms, onion, garlic and thyme in butter until tender, stirring frequently; remove from heat. Mix in flour, sour cream, soy sauce and salt.

Artichoke-Cheese Squares

You can make these ahead and freeze 'til you need them.

2 6-oz. jars artichoke hearts,
  sliced
1/2 sweet purple onion,
  finely chopped
1/4 c. bread crumbs
1-1/2 c. Cheddar cheese,
  grated

1/2 c. Parmesan cheese,
  grated
2 T. fresh parsley, chopped
1/8 t. pepper
1/8 t. dried oregano
1/8 t. hot pepper sauce
4 eggs, beaten

Drain artichokes, reserving liquid in jar. Sauté onion in liquid.
Combine bread crumbs, cheeses and seasonings in a large bowl
and add beaten eggs. Stir in artichoke hearts and onion. Pour
into a greased 13"x9" casserole dish and bake at 325 degrees
for 30 minutes. Cool 15 minutes; cut into squares. May be
served hot or cold. Makes 2 to 3 dozen.

...when daisies pied, and violets blue,
and lady-smocks all silver-white,
and cuckoo-buds of yellow hue,
do paint the meadows with delight...
-William Shakespeare, Love's Labour's Lost

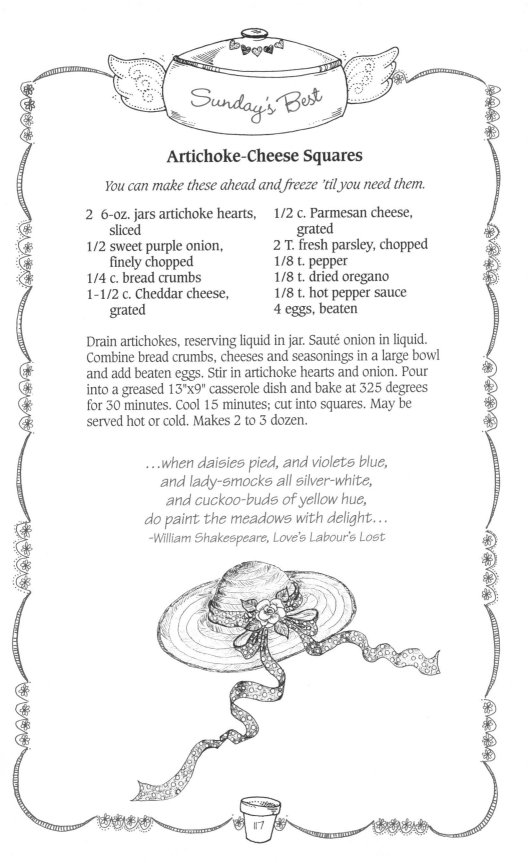

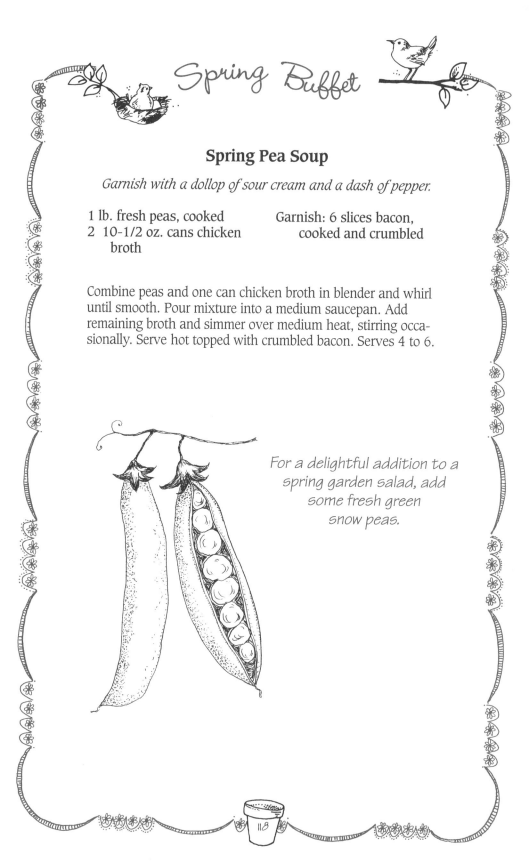

Spring Pea Soup

Garnish with a dollop of sour cream and a dash of pepper.

1 lb. fresh peas, cooked
2 10-1/2 oz. cans chicken
   broth

Garnish: 6 slices bacon,
   cooked and crumbled

Combine peas and one can chicken broth in blender and whirl until smooth. Pour mixture into a medium saucepan. Add remaining broth and simmer over medium heat, stirring occasionally. Serve hot topped with crumbled bacon. Serves 4 to 6.

For a delightful addition to a spring garden salad, add some fresh green snow peas.

Cucumber-Yogurt Salad

Cool and refreshing. Add radish roses for a pretty garnish.

2 cucumbers, peeled, halved
    and seeded
1 c. plain yogurt
1 T. olive oil

2 t. white wine vinegar
salt and pepper to taste
2 T. fresh mint, chopped
Garnish: fresh mint sprigs

Cut cucumbers into crescents. Lay on paper towels, sprinkle with salt and refrigerate for an hour to remove excess liquid. Combine the yogurt, oil, vinegar, salt. pepper and mint. Pat the cucumbers dry and toss them with yogurt mixture. Garnish with sprigs of fresh mint. Serves 4.

To make radish roses, slice off the ends of the radishes. Score one end of each radish about 3/4 of the way through, cutting the radish in a criss-cross pattern. Place in ice water for about 20 minutes to open.

Baked Country Ham

Score the fat in a diamond pattern.
Press whole cloves into the center of each diamond.

8 to 10-lb. cured Virginia ham   1/2 c. honey
2 T. prepared mustard   whole cloves
1 c. dark brown sugar, packed

Place the ham in a large Dutch oven and cover with cold water.
Let soak for 24 hours. Pour off water; cover again with cold
water and bring to a simmer over medium heat. Remove from
heat and set ham aside to cool. Preheat oven to 350 degrees.
Remove skin from the ham. Score and place in a roasting pan
on a rack. Bake about 3 to 3-1/2 hours (20 minutes per
pound). Combine mustard, brown sugar and honey in a bowl.
Spread mixture over the ham; stud with cloves. Raise oven
temperature to 450 degrees and bake ham for 30 minutes
longer. Serves 16 to 20.

The most remarkable thing
about my mother is that for
30 years she served the
family nothing but leftovers.
The original meal has never
been found.
-Calvin Trillin

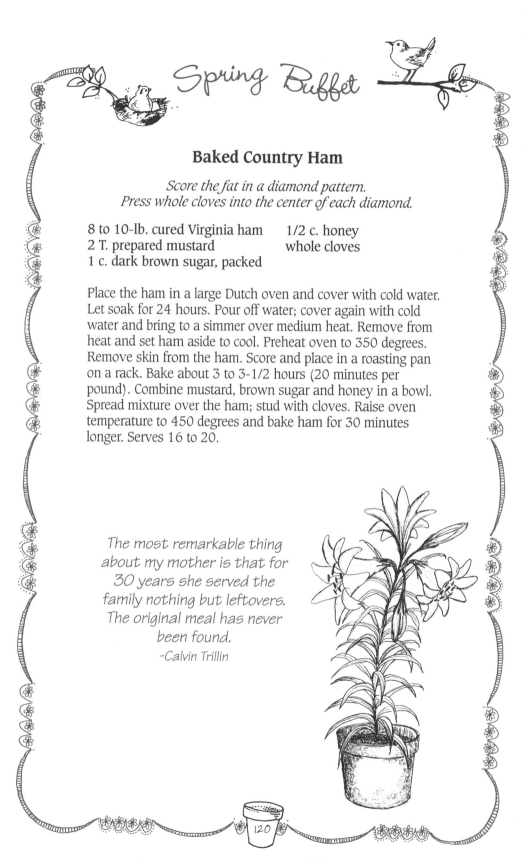

Herb-Roasted Chicken with Spring Vegetables

So simple, yet simply delicious!

3 to 3-1/2-lb. chicken
2 T. fresh rosemary, chopped
2 T. fresh marjoram, chopped

1/4 t. salt
1/4 t. pepper
Optional: fresh herb sprigs

Arrange chicken in a shallow roasting pan; loosen skin on breast and set aside. Combine herbs, salt and pepper; carefully spread half of herb mixture under loosened skin. Tuck wings under; truss legs together, if desired. Roast chicken, uncovered, at 375 degrees for one hour and 15 minutes, until chicken juices run clear when pierced or internal temperature on a meat thermometer reads 180 degrees. Serve surrounded with Spring Vegetables; garnish with fresh herb sprigs if desired. Serves 6.

Spring Vegetables:

2 c. baby carrots
1 c. frozen pearl onions,
   thawed

2 t. olive oil
10-oz. pkg. frozen baby peas,
   thawed

Combine carrots and onions in a 1-1/2 quart casserole; toss with olive oil and remaining herb mixture. Cover; place in oven when chicken has roasted for 30 minutes. Roast vegetables along with chicken for 45 minutes; add peas to casserole during final 15 minutes of roasting.

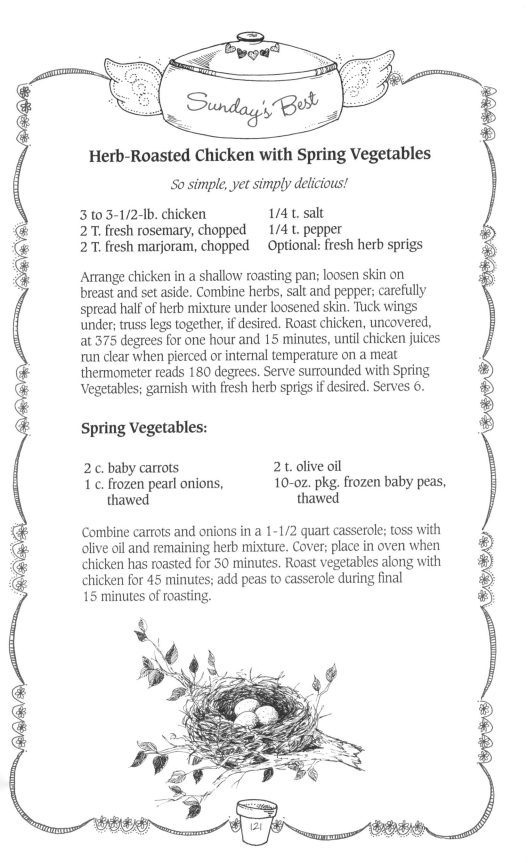

Asparagus with Tomato Vinaigrette

Just hold the asparagus by both ends and snap off the woody stems...they'll naturally break right where they should!

1 lb. fresh asparagus, trimmed	1-1/2 T. white wine vinegar
1/2 t. salt	1/2 t. honey
3 T. olive oil	2 large tomatoes, chopped

Cover the bottom of a medium saucepan with one inch of water; bring to rolling boil. Add asparagus and salt; boil for about 3 to 5 minutes, until tender. Drain. In another saucepan, heat olive oil and stir in vinegar and honey. Add tomatoes; heat through. To serve, pour vinaigrette over asparagus. Serves 4 to 6.

Rice Pilaf with Carrots

Delicious, low-fat and perfect with chicken dishes!

1 T. vegetable oil
2 c. basmati rice, uncooked
1/4 c. onion, chopped
2 cloves garlic, minced
4 c. chicken broth

1/2 t. salt
1 c. carrots, finely
  chopped
1/2 c. green onion, chopped
3 T. pine nuts, toasted

Heat oil in a medium saucepan over medium-high heat. Add rice and onion; sauté 2 minutes. Add the garlic; sauté one minute. Add broth and salt; bring to a boil. Cover, reduce heat, and simmer 7 minutes. Stir in carrots; cover and cook an additional 7 minutes or until liquid is absorbed. Remove from heat; stir in remaining ingredients. Let stand, covered, for 5 minutes, then fluff with a fork. Serves 6 to 8.

To make an Easter basket cake, decorate the top of a white layer cake with green-colored coconut. Arrange jelly beans on top, then insert both ends of a long chenille wire into the cake to form the basket "handle." Twine silk flower stems around the handle...charming!

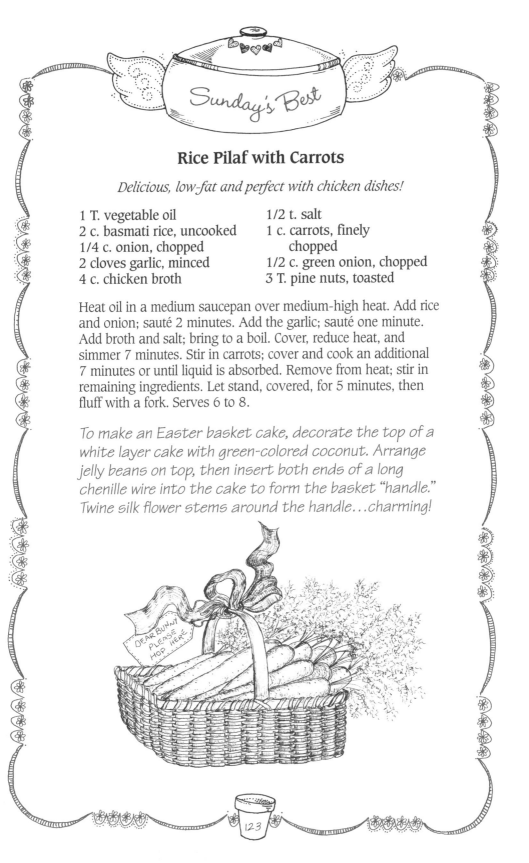

Blackberry-Peach Crisp

Top with vanilla ice cream or frozen yogurt!

Fruit:

3 lbs. peaches, pitted and cut
    into 1/2" wedges
6 c. blackberries

1-1/2 c. sugar
2 T. instant tapioca,
    uncooked

Combine all ingredients in a large bowl. Toss until sugar and tapioca are well mixed throughout; let stand 15 minutes. Transfer fruit mixture to a 13"x9" baking dish; sprinkle with topping. Bake at 375 degrees until golden and bubbly, about 50 minutes. Let cool slightly before serving. Serves 9 to 12.

Topping:

1-1/4 c. old-fashioned
    oats, uncooked
1 c. plus 2 T. brown sugar,
    packed

3/4 c. all-purpose flour
1 T. lemon zest
3/4 c. butter

Combine all ingredients except butter in a food processor. Gradually add butter and cut in, using pulse button, until a coarse crumb mixture forms.

*Eating well gives a
spectacular joy to life.*
-Elsa Schiaparelli

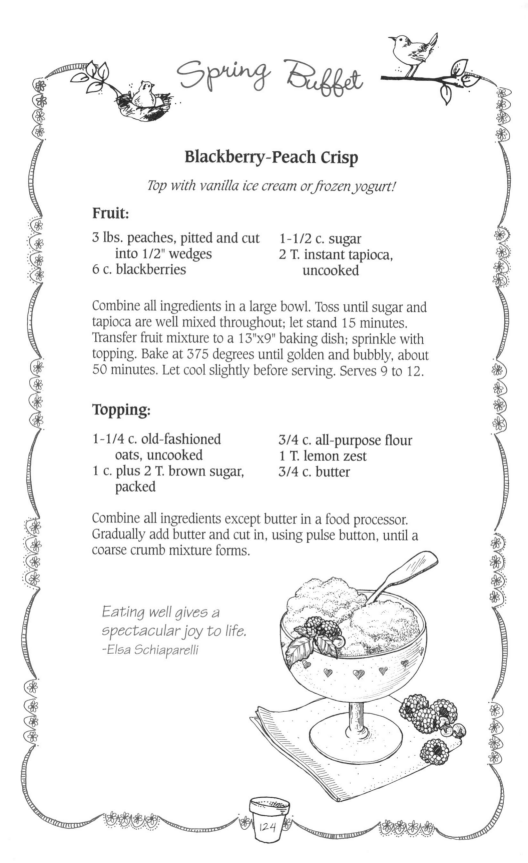

Springtime Cake Roll

Display on a pretty tray garnished with candied spring flowers.

1 c. all-purpose flour
1 t. baking powder
1/2 t. salt
3 large eggs, room
    temperature

1 t. vanilla extract
1 c. sugar
1/3 c. hot water
powdered sugar
Garnish: whipped cream

Whisk together flour, baking powder and salt in a bowl. In a separate bowl, beat eggs and vanilla with a mixer; add sugar a little at a time, beating for one more minute. Reduce mixer speed; add flour mixture to egg mixture until blended. Do not overbeat. Add hot water; mix again until smooth. Spread in a jelly-roll pan that has been lined with foil and greased. Bake for 12 to 14 minutes at 375 degrees. Loosen cake with a knife; sift powdered sugar over the top. Cover cake with a clean tea towel; invert onto a flat surface. Remove the towel and the foil, trimming off any brown edges. Roll up cake and towel together from one long edge; transfer to a wire rack and cool completely. Unroll cake and spread with filling, reserving one-third of filling for frosting. Roll cake up again and transfer to a serving platter. Frost with the reserved filling; garnish with whipped cream. Serves 10 to 15.

Orange Filling:

1/3 c. sugar
1/4 c. cornstarch
1 c. orange juice
2 T. lemon juice

1 t. orange zest
1 large egg, beaten
2 T. butter, softened

Combine sugar and cornstarch in a medium saucepan. Blend in juices and zest; cook over medium heat, stirring constantly, until thickened. Cook and stir for about 5 minutes. Remove from heat; add a portion of it to beaten egg, whisking until smooth. Return egg mixture to juice mixture; cook for a few minutes longer over low heat. Stir in butter; remove from heat and cool.

Springy things...

Eggshell Vase

Take a large raw egg and carefully pierce a small hole, about 1/4 inch in diameter, in one end with a large needle. Pierce a needle-sized hole in the other end. Blow through the smaller hole until the contents of the egg have drained out. Rinse the egg with clear water and dry. Seal the smaller hole with glue. Carefully dye the shell a pretty Easter egg color, such as lavender, buttercup yellow or soft rose. Fill the eggshell with water and a tiny bouquet of pansies. Set in a china egg cup or tiny terra cotta pot.

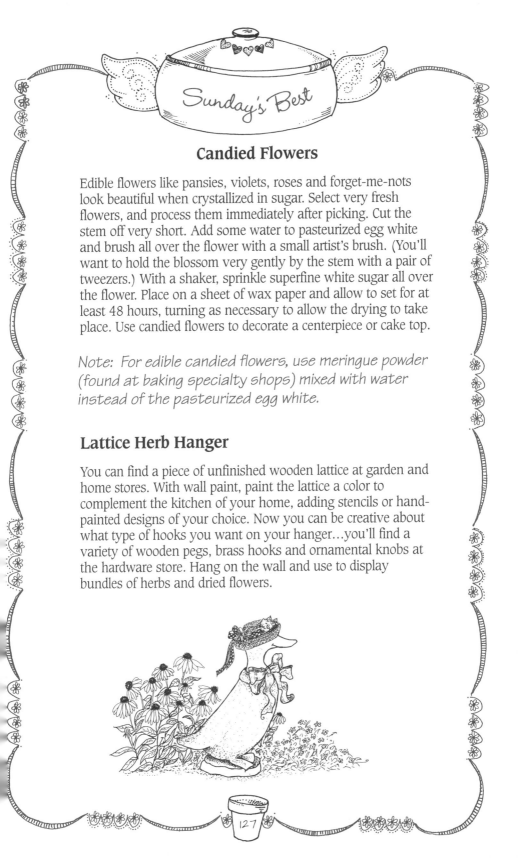

Sunday's Best

Candied Flowers

Edible flowers like pansies, violets, roses and forget-me-nots look beautiful when crystallized in sugar. Select very fresh flowers, and process them immediately after picking. Cut the stem off very short. Add some water to pasteurized egg white and brush all over the flower with a small artist's brush. (You'll want to hold the blossom very gently by the stem with a pair of tweezers.) With a shaker, sprinkle superfine white sugar all over the flower. Place on a sheet of wax paper and allow to set for at least 48 hours, turning as necessary to allow the drying to take place. Use candied flowers to decorate a centerpiece or cake top.

Note: For edible candied flowers, use meringue powder (found at baking specialty shops) mixed with water instead of the pasteurized egg white.

Lattice Herb Hanger

You can find a piece of unfinished wooden lattice at garden and home stores. With wall paint, paint the lattice a color to complement the kitchen of your home, adding stencils or hand-painted designs of your choice. Now you can be creative about what type of hooks you want on your hanger…you'll find a variety of wooden pegs, brass hooks and ornamental knobs at the hardware store. Hang on the wall and use to display bundles of herbs and dried flowers.

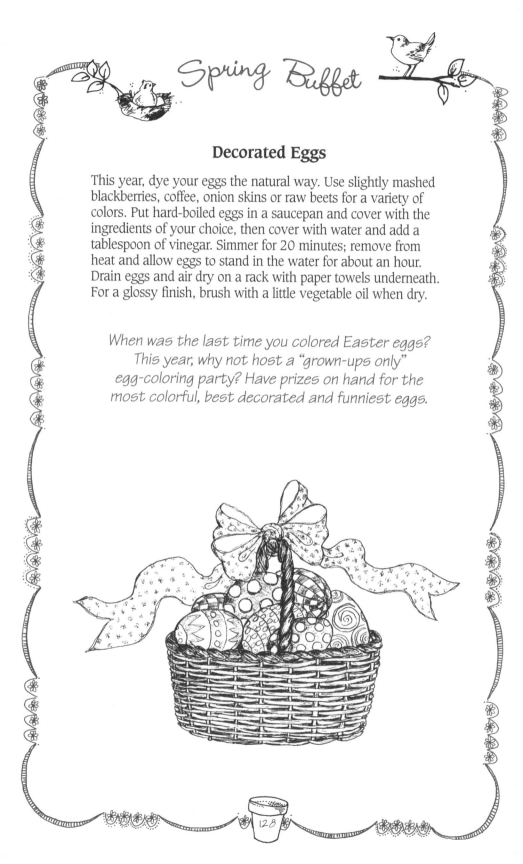

Decorated Eggs

This year, dye your eggs the natural way. Use slightly mashed blackberries, coffee, onion skins or raw beets for a variety of colors. Put hard-boiled eggs in a saucepan and cover with the ingredients of your choice, then cover with water and add a tablespoon of vinegar. Simmer for 20 minutes; remove from heat and allow eggs to stand in the water for about an hour. Drain eggs and air dry on a rack with paper towels underneath. For a glossy finish, brush with a little vegetable oil when dry.

When was the last time you colored Easter eggs? This year, why not host a "grown-ups only" egg-coloring party? Have prizes on hand for the most colorful, best decorated and funniest eggs.

Sugar Cookie Cups

Make your favorite sugar cookie recipe, cutting the cookies into 5-inch rounds. Remove the cookies from the oven a bit early, while they're still soft, and press them into custard cups. Fill with pudding or fresh berries and top with whipped cream.

Lemon Pomander Ball

Pierce several lemons all over with an awl in an evenly spaced spiral pattern. Insert whole cloves into the lemons and sprinkle with cinnamon. Arrange the lemons in a pottery bowl or basket and use as a fresh-smelling decoration for your kitchen counter or breakfast table.

Lemons will keep 3 to 4 days at room temperature. You can keep fresh lemons up to a month in the refrigerator in a sealed plastic bag.

Country Wedding

Smoked Salmon Cones with Horseradish Cream

These appetizers can be prepared ahead and refrigerated for up to 3 hours.

6 slices brown bread, thinly
    sliced
1/2 c. whipping cream
2 T. prepared horseradish

10 oz. smoked salmon,
    very thinly sliced into
    2" squares

Trim crusts off bread and cut each slice into 4 squares. Wrap in plastic and set aside. Beat cream until smooth and stiff peaks form; add horseradish. To assemble, roll salmon squares into cone shapes and place on bread squares. Using a pastry bag, fill each cone with horseradish cream. Makes about 3 dozen.

Curried Chicken Salad

The pineapple and curry add that gourmet touch.

2 c. boneless, skinless
   chicken breasts, cooked
   and diced
1 apple, peeled and cubed
1 c. pineapple, diced

1/4 c. golden raisins
1/3 c. dates, chopped
2 T. chutney
1/2 t. salt

Combine salad ingredients and refrigerate. Mix dressing with salad one hour before serving to allow flavors to blend; return to refrigerator. Makes 4 servings.

Dressing:

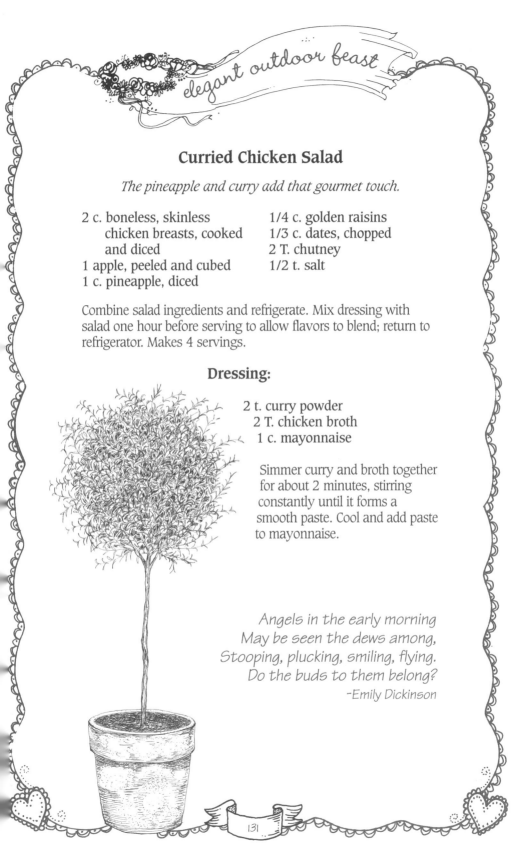

2 t. curry powder
2 T. chicken broth
1 c. mayonnaise

Simmer curry and broth together for about 2 minutes, stirring constantly until it forms a smooth paste. Cool and add paste to mayonnaise.

Angels in the early morning
May be seen the dews among,
Stooping, plucking, smiling, flying.
Do the buds to them belong?
–Emily Dickinson

Blue Cheese Cut-Out Crackers

Delicate cheese wafers with a touch of hot pepper!

1 c. all-purpose flour
7 T. crumbled blue cheese
1 large egg yolk
4 t. whipping cream

7 T. butter, softened
1/2 t. dried parsley
pinch of salt
cayenne pepper to taste

Mix all ingredients together; let rest for 30 minutes. Roll dough out to about 1/8-inch thick. Use your favorite spring shapes (flowers, teacups, wedding bells) to cut out the crackers. Bake on ungreased baking sheets at 400 degrees for 8 to 10 minutes, just until golden. Remove the delicate crackers carefully when cool. Makes 1-1/2 to 2 dozen.

Along with the fancy hors d'oeuvres, set out pretty bowls of salty toasted nuts, flavorful olives, dried figs and apricots, salsas and chips, veggies and dips, pesto and bread rounds.

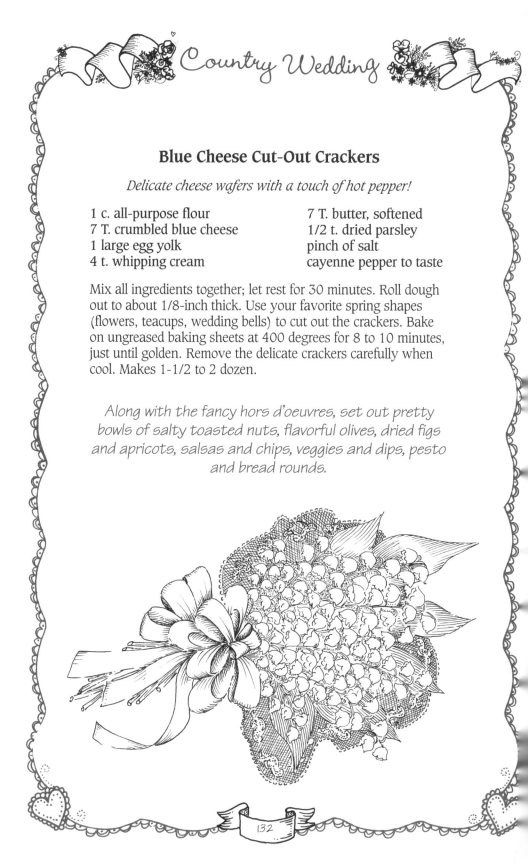

Cheese-Walnut Grape Rounds

The grapes are a nice surprise inside the cheese. Try green olives for a different taste.

8-oz. pkg. cream cheese, softened
8-oz. pkg. sharp Cheddar cheese, grated
1/2 c. butter, softened
1 T. Dijon mustard
1/2 t. Worcestershire sauce
large bunch seedless grapes
2 T. paprika
3/4 c. walnuts, chopped

Beat together cheeses, butter, mustard and Worcestershire sauce. With damp hands, form cheese mixture around individual grapes. Roll each grape in paprika, then in chopped nuts, and chill until set. Makes approximately 4 dozen.

As a wedding keepsake, decorate an unfinished blanket chest with stain or antiquing, then stencil on the names of the happy couple along with their wedding date. Cover with 2 coats of clear varnish.

Country Quiche

A clever quiche that forms its own crust while baking.

3 eggs	1/4 t. salt
1/2 c. biscuit baking mix	dash of pepper
1/2 c. butter, melted	1 c. Swiss cheese, shredded
1-1/2 c. milk	1/2 c. smoked ham, cubed

Preheat oven to 350 degrees. Place all ingredients except cheese and ham in a blender; blend well. Pour mixture into a greased 9" pie plate. Sprinkle cheese and ham on top; press gently below surface with the back of a spoon. Bake for 45 minutes. Let stand 10 minutes before cutting into wedges. Serves 6 to 8.

Berries, grapes and melon cubes make a beautiful fruit cup when served in stemmed glasses.

Blushing Pink Punch Bowl

Float pink and white rose petals and slices of lime on top.

2 c. loose hibiscus tea	1 gal. rosé wine or 3 qts.
2 qts. boiling water	white grape juice plus
1-1/2 c. honey	1 qt. red grape juice
2 qts. sparkling water	Garnish: lime slices

Tie loose tea in a cheesecloth bag and drop into boiling water. Steep, covered, about 10 minutes. Remove bag and add honey, stirring to dissolve. Cool completely and pour into a gallon container. Add sparkling water and stir. To serve, mix tea with wine or grape juices in a punch bowl over ice. Garnish with lime slices. Makes 2 gallons.

Wedding veils were originally designed to protect the bride from evil spirits. The custom of throwing the veil back after the ceremony was to ensure the groom had the right bride!

Ladyfingers

Delicate and delicious with coffee or tea.

3 eggs, separated
pinch of salt
1/8 t. cream of tartar
1/2 c. sugar, divided
1 t. vanilla extract

pinch of nutmeg
1/8 t. almond extract
1/2 c. all-purpose flour
2 T. cornstarch
1/2 c. powdered sugar

Beat egg whites until foamy. Add salt and cream of tartar; beat again until soft peaks are formed. Beat in 1/4 cup sugar, one teaspoon at a time. Continue to beat for one minute on high speed. In a separate bowl, beat egg yolks and add vanilla, nutmeg, almond extract and remaining sugar. Beat well until light in color. Pour over egg whites and fold together. Sift flour and cornstarch together; sprinkle gradually over the egg mixture. Fold in very gently with a spatula, so mixture is very light. Transfer half the batter into a pastry bag with a 3/4-inch plain tip. Pipe the batter onto a greased baking sheet, making the ladyfingers about 4 inches long by 1-1/2 inches wide. Dust with powdered sugar. Bake 20 minutes at 300 degrees, until golden. Turn off heat; leave ladyfingers in oven for another 5 minutes. Remove from sheet and cool on rack. Makes one to 1-1/2 dozen.

A heart-shaped basket makes a beautiful centerpiece. Fill with white violets, roses and baby's breath.

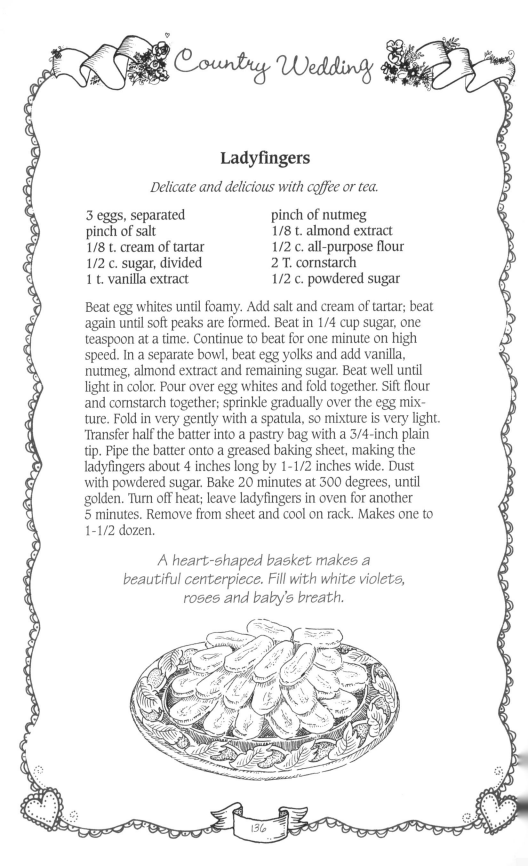

Fudge-Topped Cherry Hearts

Prepared ingredients make these quick & easy to make!

8-oz. pkg. frozen puff pastry
    sheets, thawed
3/4 c. cherry pie filling

8 t. fudge ice cream
    topping
Garnish: chopped almonds

Preheat oven to 375 degrees. Unfold pastry onto lightly floured
surface. Using a heart-shaped cookie cutter, cut pastry into
8 hearts. Place hearts on an ungreased baking sheet and bake
for 15 to 18 minutes, until golden. Let cool and split hearts
horizontally. Spoon cherry pie filling into each heart and replace
tops. To serve, heat fudge topping until smooth and drizzle over
hearts. Sprinkle with nuts and serve immediately. Serves 8.

Love is an irresistible desire to be
irresistibly desired.
-Robert Frost

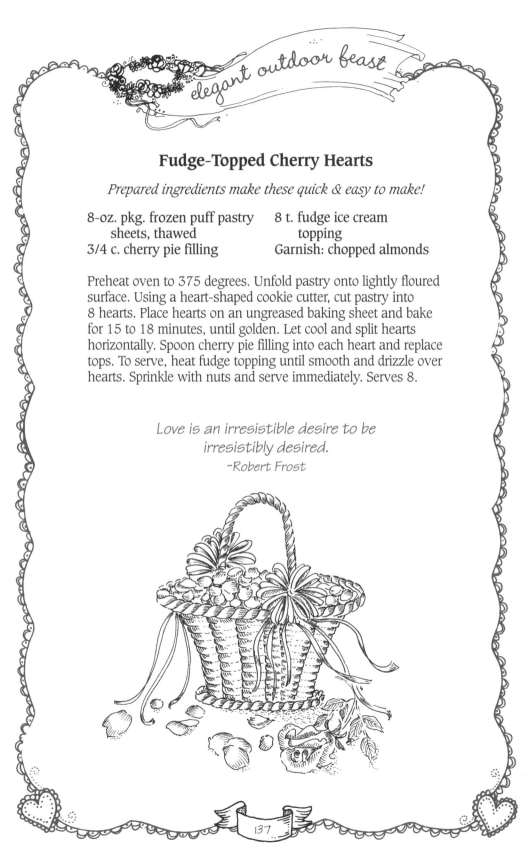

Country Wedding

Memorable weddings...

Table Decorating Ideas

For a country wedding, cover your buffet table in antique lace.
You can use a coordinating color underneath for a gentle hint
of color. Fill a large gathering basket with Queen Anne's lace,
violets, white cosmos and black-eyed Susans. If your wedding
party will extend into nighttime, be sure to place lots of white
pillar candles in sparkling glass containers...canning jars, jelly
jars, brandy snifters and hurricane lamps. Keep bugs away
with citronella candles attached to garden stakes and planted
all around the area.

Sponge Painted Pots

Giant terra cotta pots look beautiful at a country wedding. You
can sponge paint them in white, mustard or any combination
of your wedding colors. Fill the pots with impatiens, geraniums
or your flowers of choice. Wrap wide wired ribbons around the
pots and make huge bows. Line the pots up at the entrance,
flank the buffet tables...the ideas are endless!

Beautiful Cakes

A wedding cake can be as individual as you are. In times past, wedding cakes were white with fluffy white frosting and a little bride and groom on top. Today, you can select your favorite flavor, whether it be chocolate-raspberry, carrot, spice, almond, mocha, orange or lemon. You can decorate the top of the cake with fresh flowers, berries, lemon leaves, satin ribbons, chocolate curls, white chocolate molded flowers or baby's breath. Many couples today are incorporating hobbies and interests into their cakes…for example, instead of a bride and groom on top, they may have a little pair of tennis racquets, skis and poles, miniature gardening tools or any symbol that is most significant to them. Display your cake on a beautiful silver platter, in a large square basket, on a big bread board or a fabric-covered heart. Decorate base of cake with fresh flowers and greenery to match your bridal bouquet.

Dainty little maiden, whither would you wander?
Whither from this pretty home, the home where
mother dwells?
Far and far away, said the
dainty little maiden,
All among the gardens,
auriculas, anemones,
Roses and lilies
and Canterbury-bells.
  -Alfred Lord Tennyson

Table Favors

A gift of sweets is a tradition that's easy to accomplish. Select a candy...sugar-coated almonds, lemon drops, jelly beans, mints or chocolate-covered disks, depending on your color scheme and tastes. Place a handful of the candy into a 12-inch diameter circle of tulle. Gather up the ends and tie with satin ribbons to complement the table setting.

Floral Bath Oils

A beautiful gift for your bridesmaids...whisk together 6 ounces of glycerine with 2 ounces of floral perfume oil. Select rose, lavender or violet, for example. Pour oil into a pretty glass bottle and cover with a cork or tight-fitting lid. Tie a ribbon around the top and attach a little tag with the instructions: "Add one teaspoon to a hot bath, and relax!"

Lacy Ring Pillow

It's so easy to make a fancy little ring pillow out of lacy handkerchiefs! Simply stitch 2 hankies together on 3 sides. Stuff with cotton batting and sew up the open side. Add a wide ribbon trim all around the edge...choose white or a coordinating color. Attach a little ribbon loop to the middle, fastened with hook and loop fabric, for keeping the rings safe and sound.

Framed Invitation

Set the invitation on a standard-sized piece of matboard with enough margin to add border items. Save and press some of the flowers from the centerpiece, bits of ribbon, lace and a small photo of the bride and groom. Surround the invitation with these items and glue into place, then insert into a ready-made frame.

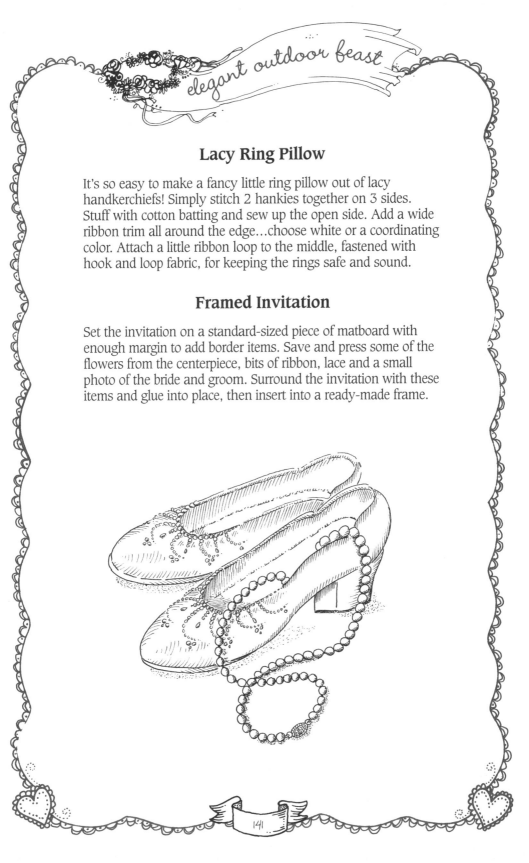

Especially for Mom

Sautéed Tomatoes with Tarragon

Garnish with fresh tarragon.

1 T. butter
1 T. olive oil
2 large tomatoes, sliced
    1/2" thick

1 T. fresh tarragon, chopped
pepper to taste
dash of cayenne pepper

Heat butter and oil in a large iron skillet over medium heat. Add tomatoes and sprinkle with seasonings. After 2 to 3 minutes, tomatoes should be golden. Flip them over and cook through. Serves 2 to 4.

The more passions and desires one has, the more ways one has of being happy.
-Charlotte-Catherine

TO MOM
I LOVE YOU

Easy Red Potato Frittata

*Mom will love this for breakfast with a toasted English muffin
and fresh berries on the side.*

3 egg whites	1/2 c. new redskin potatoes,
1 egg	diced
2 T. fresh chives, chopped	1/4 c. red pepper, chopped
and divided	1/2 c. broccoli flowerets
1/8 t. salt	1/3 c. water
1/8 t. pepper	1/2 t. vegetable oil

In a mixing bowl, beat together egg whites, egg, one tablespoon
chives, salt and pepper. Spray skillet with non-stick vegetable
spray; sauté potatoes until golden. Add red pepper, broccoli and
water; cover and cook about 3 minutes, until potatoes are
tender. Uncover and cook until liquid has cooked away; add oil
and toss until well-coated. Add egg mixture. Let cook until eggs
begin to set, then stir well. Cover and continue cooking until
eggs are set, but still moist on top. Uncover and place under
heated broiler until crisp and golden on top. Serve immediately,
topped with remaining chives. Makes 2 to 4 servings.

*Cherish all your happy moments; they make
a fine cushion for old age.*
-Christopher Morley

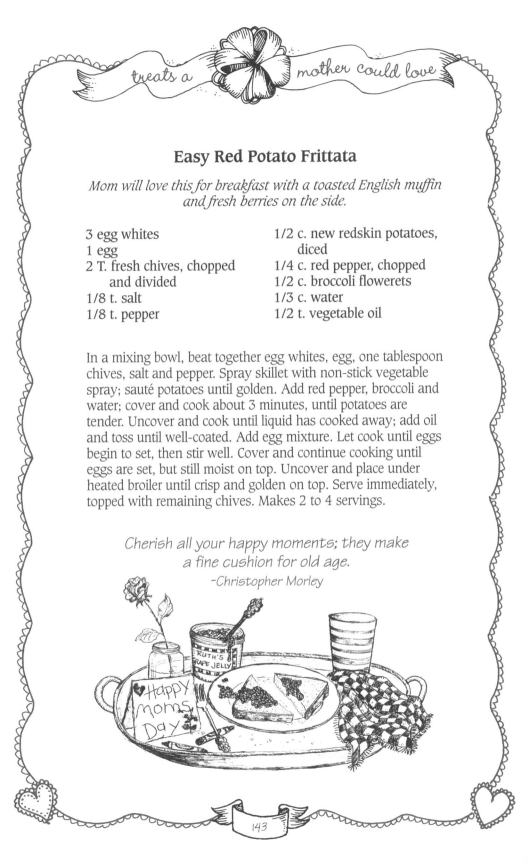

Herb Omelet

Fresh garden herbs add a delicious taste to this special omelet.

2 T. butter
1/4 c. mushrooms, sliced
5 eggs, beaten with 1 t.
   water
1/2 t. fresh tarragon, finely
   chopped
1/2 t. fresh dill, finely
   chopped

1/2 t. fresh chives, finely
   chopped
salt and pepper to taste
1/2 tomato, chopped
1/2 c. Cheddar cheese,
   shredded and divided
Garnish: fresh dill sprigs

Melt butter in a large sauté pan over medium heat. Sauté
mushrooms for one minute. In a large bowl, combine eggs,
water, herbs, salt and pepper and whisk briskly for at least
30 seconds. When a drop of water sizzles in the pan, add egg
mixture. As eggs set, gently run a spatula through them several
times so uncooked egg reaches the bottom. Add tomato and
1/4 cup cheese to the top of the omelet. When bottom is golden,
flip half the omelet over on itself. Transfer to a plate and sprinkle
with more cheese. Garnish with fresh dill. Serves 2.

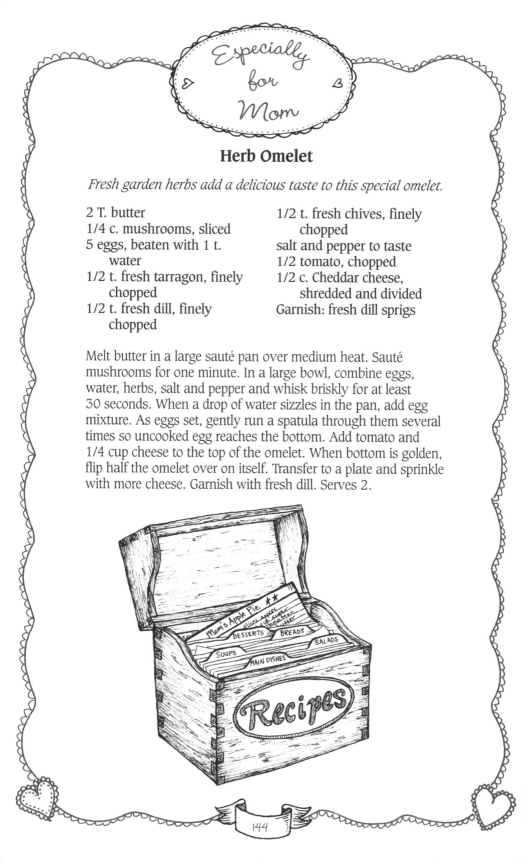

Orange Muffins

Zesty and elegant. Place in a basket with a lace doily and a fresh bouquet of daffodils.

1-3/4 c. all-purpose flour	1 large egg
1-1/2 t. baking powder	1 t. vanilla extract
1/2 t. salt	2/3 c. milk
6 T. butter, softened	2 to 3 T. orange zest
2/3 c. sugar	Optional: fresh violets

Preheat oven to 375 degrees. In a large bowl, combine flour, baking powder and salt; set aside. In another bowl, beat together butter and sugar at medium speed. Blend in egg and vanilla and beat until fluffy. Add flour mixture and milk alternately to this mixture, beating until just combined. Fold in orange zest; fill greased muffin cups. Bake for about 25 minutes, until tester comes out clean. Cool slightly and garnish with fresh violets, if desired. Makes 10 to 12.

Where there is great love, there are always miracles.
-Willa Cather

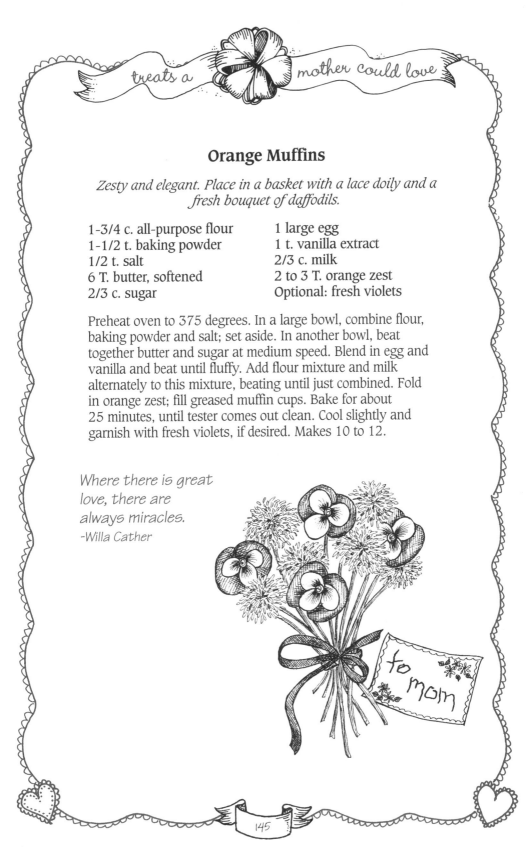

Strawberry-Spinach Salad

Fresh and elegant!

8 c. spinach, torn
1/2 c. strawberries, hulled
  and halved
2 c. cantaloupe balls
2 T. raspberry white wine
  vinegar

2 T. seedless raspberry jam
1 T. honey
2 t. olive oil
1/4 c. macadamia nuts,
  chopped

In a large bowl, toss spinach, strawberries and cantaloupe. In a smaller bowl, whisk together vinegar, jam, honey and olive oil. Drizzle over salad and toss. Top with nuts. Serves 6.

Garnish a salad with strawberry fans. Cut 4 or 5 very thin slices through the berries from tip to hull, leaving the hull intact. Fan out the berries and arrange on the salad plate.

Mother's Luscious Chocolate Cake

Dust the top with powdered sugar over a lacy paper doily.
Leaves a beautiful image on top!

2 c. all-purpose flour
2 t. baking soda
1/2 t. salt
1/2 c. butter
2 c. sugar
3 large eggs
1-1/2 t. vanilla extract

1/2 c. unsweetened
   chocolate, melted and
   cooled
4-oz. pkg. instant chocolate
   pudding mix
1 c. sour cream
1/2 c. milk

Preheat oven to 350 degrees. Sift together flour, baking soda
and salt. In another larger bowl, beat together butter and sugar;
add eggs and beat until light and fluffy. Beat in vanilla and
chocolate, alternating with flour mixture, pudding mix and sour
cream. Stir in milk to thin batter; pour into an 8" springform
pan. Bake for 50 to 55 minutes or until cake tester comes out
clean. Cool cake in pan for 10 minutes, then turn out onto rack
and cool completely. Serves 6 to 8.

Almond Tea

Make a pot especially for Mom, to go with her chocolate cake.

3 teabags
6 c. water, divided
1 c. sugar or equivalent
    sweetener

2/3 c. lemon juice
2 t. almond extract
1 t. vanilla extract

Steep teabags in 2 cups boiling water for about 10 minutes. In a separate pan, bring 4 cups water to a boil and add sugar. Let simmer for 5 minutes, then add lemon juice, almond and vanilla. Combine the mixture with the brewed tea. May be served hot or iced. Makes about 2 quarts.

Gift ideas for Mothers' Day...

Ivy Topiary

You will need:

1 yd. heavy-gauge wire	6" terra cotta pot
needle-nose pliers	potting soil
wire cutter	2 small ivy plants
small pebbles	jute

Bend the wire into a circle; use pliers to twist the ends together. The end piece should be about 5 inches long, or long enough to reach the bottom of the pot. Shape the loop into a circle. Put pebbles into the bottom of the pot, fill pot halfway with potting soil, and plant your ivies in the center of the pot. Make sure shoots are growing outward in opposite directions. Cover the plants with additional soil and tap the pot to settle the roots. Water generously, allowing excess water to drain. Place wire topiary form in the pot between the plants so it is firmly in the soil. Gently wrap the shoots around the twisted wire and onto both sides of the form. Temporarily tie the shoots in place with small pieces of jute. Then watch your topiary grow!

Gift Coupon Book

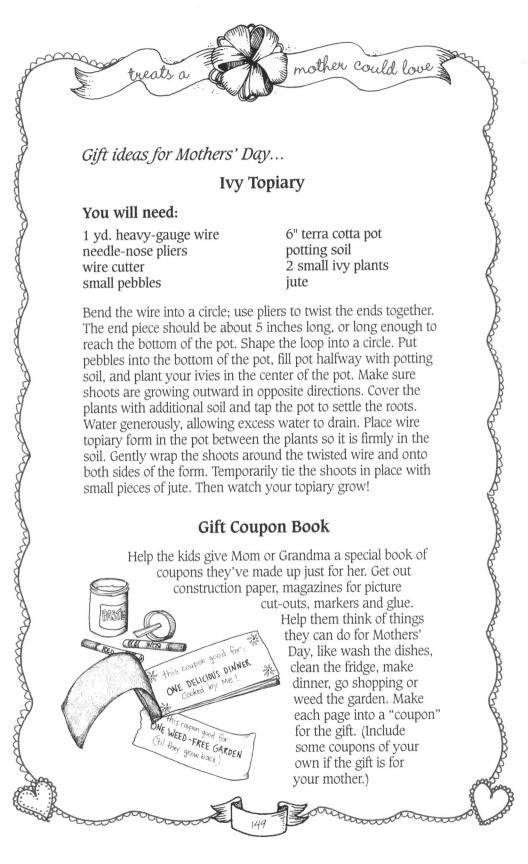

Help the kids give Mom or Grandma a special book of coupons they've made up just for her. Get out construction paper, magazines for picture cut-outs, markers and glue. Help them think of things they can do for Mothers' Day, like wash the dishes, clean the fridge, make dinner, go shopping or weed the garden. Make each page into a "coupon" for the gift. (Include some coupons of your own if the gift is for your mother.)

Especially for Mom

Cookie Baking Box

Decorate the outside of a sturdy gift box with pretty fabric cut-outs coated with craft glue. Fill the box with cookie cutters, a recipe book like Gooseberry Patch's **Christmas Cookies**, sugar sprinkles, icing bag and tips and chocolate chips. A thoughtful gift for the mom who loves to bake!

Tea Basket

For the mother who's a tea drinker, fill a basket with some teatime favorites…a special mug or cup, flavored and herbal teabags, a silver teaspoon, sugar cubes or packets, even a tiny book of tea.

Lavender Dryer Sachet

A great gift for Mom…can also be used as a drawer or closet sachet. You'll need:

1/4 yd. cotton fabric
needle and thread
lavender buds

cotton ball
decorative ribbon

Cut the fabric into a rectangle, double heart or double circle. With the fabric wrong-side up, turn the edges over 1/4 inch and iron the edges flat. Fold the fabric in half to form your basic shape. Stitch all the way around the shape, leaving a small opening for stuffing. Turn the bag right side out and fill with as many lavender buds as possible, packing tightly. Place the cotton ball inside last, next to the opening, so no buds can escape. (For extra scent, you can put a drop of lavender oil on the cotton ball.) Stitch the opening shut…if you like, you can make a drawstring stitch so bag can be reopened. Make a bow with the ribbon and tie it to the sachet, sewing it on securely.

Molded Chocolate Cups

Mom will love them! You'll need a cup of semi-sweet chocolate chips and 8 paper cupcake liners. Place the chocolate in the top of a double boiler over hot water. When chocolate is partially melted, remove from heat and let it stand to melt completely. Dip a small brush into the chocolate and paint the inside of the cupcake liners, building up the sides thickly so the cups won't break when paper is removed. Turn onto a baking sheet and refrigerate until hardened. Carefully peel off the paper; store cups in a cool area. Fill cups with Mom's favorite…pudding, ice cream, melted chocolate and peanuts, chocolate mousse, whipped cream and crushed cookies or candies.

Giant Heart Cookie

Mix up a batch of your favorite chocolate chip cookie dough. Spread the dough into an 8" or 9" heart-shaped baking pan (dough should cover the bottom of the pan and be about 1/4-inch thick). Bake as usual, until golden brown. Allow to cool slightly and turn your giant cookie out of the pan onto a cooling rack. When completely cool, pipe colorful icing around the edge and write a special message inside.

The greatest lessons I have ever learned were at my mother's knees…all that I am, or hope to be, I owe to my angel mother.
-Abraham Lincoln

Garden Party

Tomato Bruschetta

Add thin slices of sweet yellow or purple onion, if you like.

12-oz. loaf Italian bread, cut in 1" diagonal slices
1/2 pt. cherry tomatoes, quartered
1 small yellow pepper, chopped
3 T. olive oil, divided
3 cloves garlic (1 minced, 2 halved)
1 T. fresh basil, chopped
2 T. Parmesan cheese, freshly grated

Place bread directly on grill (or on broiler rack in oven); lightly toast both sides for about 2 minutes. In small bowl, combine tomatoes, pepper, one tablespoon olive oil, minced garlic and basil. Rub one side of each toasted bread slice with halved garlic cloves and then brush with remaining olive oil. Spoon heaping spoonfuls of tomato mixture onto each slice and sprinkle with cheese. Makes 8 servings.

A garden party is the perfect occasion for swapping seeds and cuttings. Give your guests each a little potted cutting as a party favor.

Artichoke-Red Pepper Dip

Surround this dip with an array of fresh vegetables...carrots, radishes, celery and peppers.

1/2 c. mayonnaise
1/2 c. sour cream
1/2 c. artichoke hearts, chopped
1/3 c. roasted red peppers

1 garlic clove, minced
2 T. fresh basil, chopped
1/8 t. dried oregano
1/8 t. salt

Blend all ingredients together. Cover and chill for one hour to allow flavors to blend. Makes 1-1/2 cups.

Oh! The things which happened in that garden!
If you have never had a garden,
you cannot understand, and if you have had
a garden, you will know that it would take a
whole book to describe all the things that
came to pass there.
-Frances Hodgson Burnett,
The Secret Garden

Sesame Asparagus

*For best results, use an iron skillet. Serve chilled with
a dash of fresh lemon juice.*

2 T. peanut oil	2 t. soy sauce
1 lb. asparagus, trimmed	pepper to taste
2 T. shallots, minced	dash of lemon juice
1 T. sesame seed	

Heat oil in a skillet over medium-high heat; add asparagus in a
single layer. Cook asparagus for about 4 minutes, then turn and
cook 3 more minutes. Asparagus will be slightly browned. Add
the shallots and sesame seed and cook, tossing the asparagus in
the mixture, until the shallots are transparent. Add soy sauce
and pepper, then transfer to a plate and sprinkle with lemon
juice. Serves 4.

*Asparagus is best when eaten freshly picked. You can
store it for a few days in the refrigerator wrapped in a
plastic bag. Don't clean until ready to cook.*

Minted Pea Salad

Can be prepared and served immediately or refrigerated.

4 c. fresh peas, blanched, or
   16-oz. pkg. frozen peas, thawed
1/4 lb. slice smoked ham, chopped
1/2 c. fresh mint, chopped

1/2 c. mayonnaise
1/4 c. rice wine vinegar
1 t. fresh dill, chopped

Combine peas, ham and mint in mixing bowl. In another bowl, combine mayonnaise, vinegar and dill. Add dressing to peas and toss together. Makes 4 to 6 servings.

They say spring has come when you can put your foot on 3 daisies.
-Folk wisdom

Greek Salad in a Pita Pocket

*You can make a delicious sandwich out of almost any
vegetable salad with tasty pita bread.*

1 red pepper, thinly sliced
1/2 avocado, pitted and
   sliced
1/4 sweet red onion, thinly
   sliced
5 to 6 black Greek olives,
   pitted and sliced
crumbled feta cheese to taste

1 t. garlic, crushed
fresh dill to taste, chopped
1/2 t. dried oregano
oil & vinegar salad
   dressing to taste
4 rounds pita bread,
   split

Gently toss all salad ingredients with the dressing. Stuff into
pita pockets. Serves 4.

Creamy Raspberry Smoothie

Cool, refreshing and colorful.

1-3/4 c. raspberries
1-1/4 c. white grape juice
1-1/2 c. raspberry sherbet
1/4 c. water

1 T. lemon juice
10 ice cubes
fresh mint sprigs

Place raspberries and grape juice in blender and blend until smooth. Strain the mixture. Add sherbet, water and lemon juice in blender container; cover and process until smooth. Add ice cubes; process until frothy. Garnish with fresh mint sprigs and serve immediately. Makes 3 cups.

About berries...

- Berries are best cleaned by rinsing gently in a colander using lukewarm water. Gently pat dry with a soft cloth.
- Be extra careful cleaning raspberries and blackberries, as they are very delicate.
- Don't wash berries until you're ready to serve them.
- Leave the hulls intact when you wash them.
- If you can't use fresh berries immediately, line a large plate with a paper towel and arrange berries so they're not touching. They'll keep up to 3 days, although refrigerating does cause berries to lose some of their flavor.

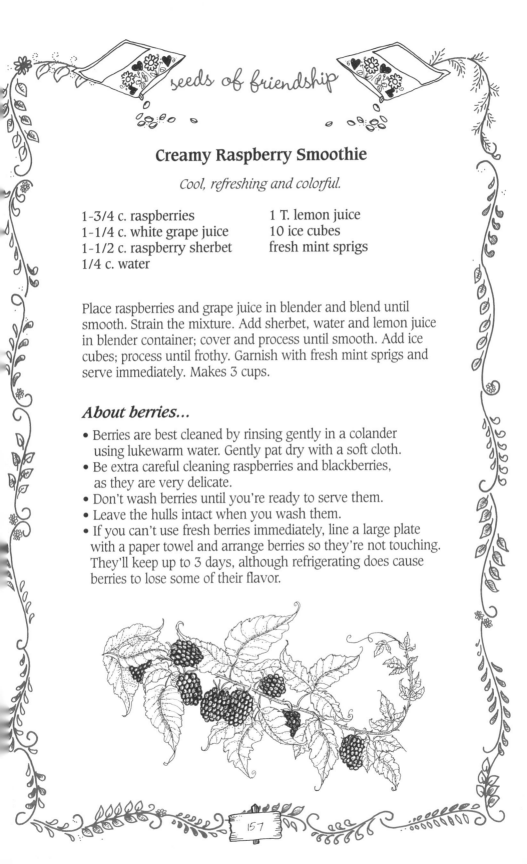

Violet Layer Cake

Freshly picked violets look pretty around the base of the cake.

White Cake:

1/2 c. butter, softened	1-1/4 c. cold water
1-2/3 c. sugar	1 t. vanilla extract
2-1/2 c. cake flour, sifted	4 egg whites, beaten
1/4 t. salt	2 t. baking powder

Cream butter and sugar with a mixer. Sift flour and salt together; add to butter mixture, alternating with water. Add vanilla. In a separate bowl, beat egg whites until frothy. Add baking powder gradually, continuing to beat until stiff. Fold egg whites into the batter. Pour into 2 greased and floured 8" round cake pans; bake at 350 degrees for 25 minutes. Touch center of cake to test for doneness; when it springs back, it is done. Frost both layers of cake and stack. Scatter frosted violets over the top of the cake. Serves 8 to 10.

Buttercream Frosting:

1/2 c. butter, softened	2 T. milk
1-1/2 c. powdered sugar	1/2 t. vanilla extract

Beat all ingredients together with a mixer until smooth and thick. Add more sugar if frosting is too thin.

Frosted Violets:

With a small artist's brush, gently brush a mixture of pasteurized egg white and water on freshly rinsed and dried violets. Dip in superfine sugar.

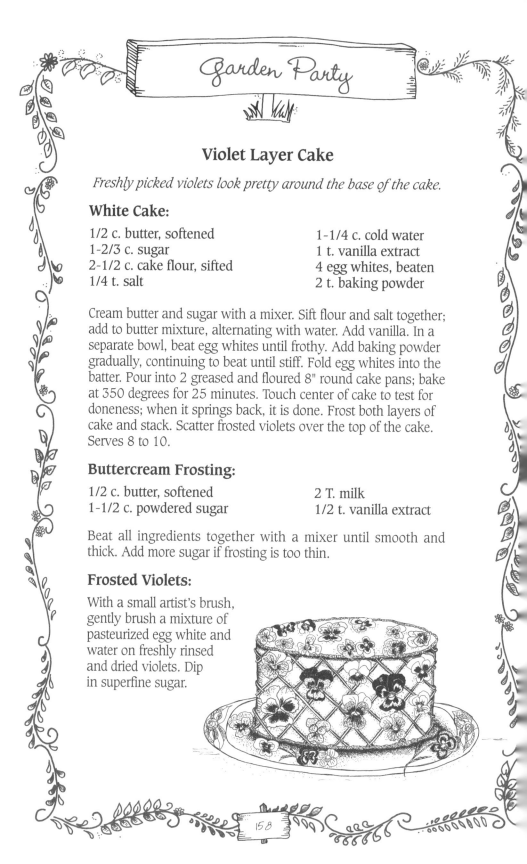

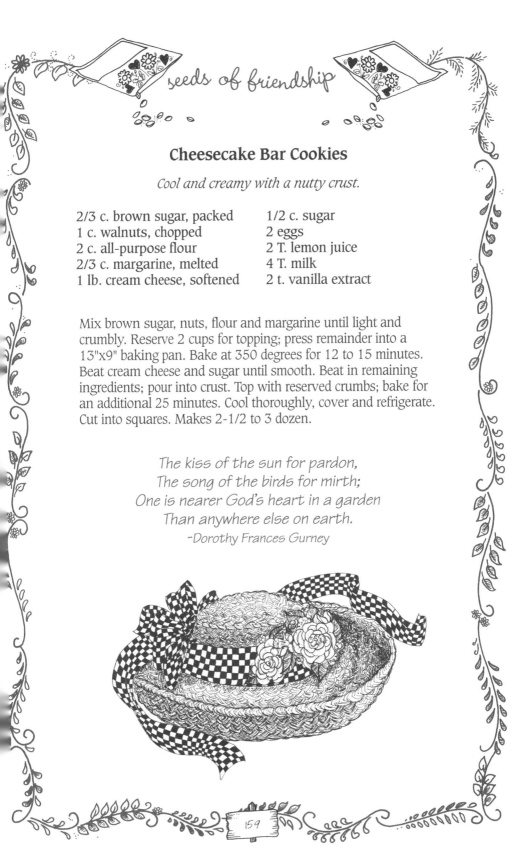

Cheesecake Bar Cookies

Cool and creamy with a nutty crust.

2/3 c. brown sugar, packed	1/2 c. sugar
1 c. walnuts, chopped	2 eggs
2 c. all-purpose flour	2 T. lemon juice
2/3 c. margarine, melted	4 T. milk
1 lb. cream cheese, softened	2 t. vanilla extract

Mix brown sugar, nuts, flour and margarine until light and crumbly. Reserve 2 cups for topping; press remainder into a 13"x9" baking pan. Bake at 350 degrees for 12 to 15 minutes. Beat cream cheese and sugar until smooth. Beat in remaining ingredients; pour into crust. Top with reserved crumbs; bake for an additional 25 minutes. Cool thoroughly, cover and refrigerate. Cut into squares. Makes 2-1/2 to 3 dozen.

The kiss of the sun for pardon,
The song of the birds for mirth;
One is nearer God's heart in a garden
Than anywhere else on earth.
–Dorothy Frances Gurney

Fresh ideas...

Floral Spoons

Collect pretty, deep-bowled spoons and ladles from flea markets to make this easy craft. They make beautiful party favors! You'll need:

florist's foam
vintage spoons
tacky glue
thin satin ribbon

small dried flower blossoms
such as purple statice,
baby's breath, globe
amaranth and lavender

Cut a small amount of florist's foam to fill the well of each spoon. (A melon baller works perfectly to cut the foam for a regular tablespoon.) Glue foam firmly into the spoon; let dry overnight. When dry, push dried flowers into the base, completely covering the foam. Tie a ribbon bow onto the spoon handles. Place spoons at individual place settings.

Decorated Trays

Here's a fun and functional gift that everyone will love to take home. Découpage small unfinished wooden trays with vintage seed packs and labels. Use the trays at place settings, along with small notebooks and pencils for garden planning. They make the lunch more portable, and will serve as a charming remembrance of your garden party.

Sweet Butter Blossoms

These look beautiful on a glass platter or individual bread plates. Rinse 1/4 cup of your favorite edible flower petals...violets or nasturtiums work well. If you wish, add finely chopped dill or chives. Soften 1/2 cup of butter to room temperature and beat, combining with herbs and flowers. Pipe butter onto wax paper through a cookie press using a star tip. Chill until firm, then transfer to serving platter or plates.

Garden Party

Forced Hyacinths

Forcing hyacinths was such a popular practice in Victorian days, special hyacinth glasses were made just for that purpose and can be found in many antique shops. Forcing is easy to do; just be sure you get good-quality bulbs and keep them in a cool place (damp sand is perfect) until ready to plant. Choose a container that will support the bulb slightly above the water and have plenty of room for the roots; if you can't find a real hyacinth glass, a bud vase, jelly jar or little glass pitcher will usually work well. Fill with lukewarm water, making sure the water just touches the bottom of the bulb. Change the water about twice a week. Keep in a cool, dark place for 3 to 4 weeks, or until roots and leaves begin to show. Then move to a warmer, sunnier spot. Turn the container occasionally for even sunlight exposure. Hyacinths take about 6 weeks to blossom, so be patient!

Celebrate Summer

All-American Cookout

Grilled Garlic Burgers

Serve a platter of fresh lettuce and slices of vine-ripened tomato, pickle and onion for toppings.

1-3/4 lbs. ground beef
2 T. garlic, minced
1/2 c. onion, finely chopped
2 t. salt
2 t. pepper
6 oz. fresh horseradish,
   peeled and shredded

1 T. vegetable oil
2 T. mustard
1/2 c. plus 2 T. catsup
2 T. sour cream
4 onion buns

In a mixing bowl, mix ground beef, garlic, onion, salt and pepper. Shape into 4 patties. Sprinkle with horseradish and press into meat. Coat grill or a large skillet with oil and cook burgers for 4 to 5 minutes per side. While cooking, mix together mustard, catsup and sour cream. Top with catsup mixture and serve on grilled buns. Serves 4.

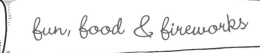

Lime & Ginger Grilled Salmon

Arrange slices of fresh lemon and lime alongside.

2-lb. salmon fillet, skinned
   and boned
2 T. fresh ginger, minced
2 T. lime zest
1/2 t. salt

1/2 t. pepper
1/2 t. lime juice
2 T. butter, melted, or
   olive oil

Heat grill. Sprinkle salmon with ginger, lime zest, salt and pepper. In a small bowl, combine lime juice and butter; brush salmon with mixture. Grill about 5 minutes per side, or until salmon flakes easily. Makes 4 servings.

Here's a foolproof method for grilling fish that'll keep it from falling apart and disappearing into the grill...make a "boat" out of a double thickness of aluminum foil. Place the fish fillet (no more than one inch thick) in the center of the foil and turn up the edges all the way around to catch drippings. Cook the fish, boat and all, uncovered on top of the grill for 8 to 10 minutes or until fish flakes easily with a fork. There's no need to turn the fish. To serve, top fish with some of the juices in the boat.

All-American Cookout

Creamed Peas

Salmon and fresh peas are a traditional New England Independence Day dish.

1 T. butter
1 T. vegetable oil
1 c. onion, finely chopped

4 c. peas, freshly shelled
3 T. whipping cream
salt and pepper to taste

Melt butter with oil in a large saucepan over low heat. Add onion and cook until tender and golden, about 15 minutes. Add peas and just enough water to reach the top of the peas. Bring to a simmer; cover and cook about 15 minutes, or until peas are very tender. Add cream and cook until the liquid thickens into a sauce, about 5 or 6 minutes. Season to taste. Serves 6 to 8.

Spray paint a small brown paper bag bright red. Arrange little flags in a wide-mouthed jar and put inside the bag. Fold the top of the bag down 2 or 3 times and tie with a ribbon, raffia or strip of home-spun. Makes a star-spangled table decoration!

Grilled Vegetable Skewers

Choose the veggies you like...all are delicious grilled!

summer squash, quartered
zucchini, quartered
onions, halved
eggplant, quartered

red or yellow peppers, halved
whole mushrooms
tomatoes, quartered
scallions, trimmed

Brush vegetables with marinade. Skewer and cook on the grill, continuing to baste while cooking. Squash, zucchini, onions and eggplant will take longer to cook. Add peppers, mushrooms, tomatoes and scallions last; grill until tender.

Marinade:

1/2 c. butter, melted
1/2 c. lemon juice

1 T. fresh basil, chopped
pepper to taste

Blend together in a small bowl.

The second day of July, 1776...ought to be solemnized with pomp and parade, with shows, games, sports, guns, bells, bonfires, and illuminations, from one end of this continent to the other, from this time forward forevermore.

-John Adams, July 3, 1776 letter to Abigail Adams

Summer Vegetable Salad

A "just-right" medley of color, crunch and spice!

1 c. asparagus, chopped	2 t. balsamic vinegar
1 c. tomatoes, chopped	2 T. olive oil
1 c. zucchini, shredded	7 dashes hot pepper sauce
1 c. red pepper, diced	

Cook asparagus in a small amount of boiling water until crisp-tender; drain. In a salad bowl, combine asparagus, tomatoes, zucchini and red pepper. In another bowl, whisk together vinegar, oil and hot pepper sauce. Combine dressing with salad just before serving. Serves 6 to 8.

Blue Cheese Potato Salad

Try a variation of this recipe with new redskin potatoes...no need to peel. Garnish with fresh dill.

8 c. potatoes, peeled, boiled and cubed	1/2 t. celery seed
	2 t. salt
1/2 c. scallions, chopped	1/4 t. pepper
1/2 c. celery, chopped	1/2 c. crumbled blue cheese
2 T. fresh parsley, chopped	2 c. sour cream
1/2 c. almond slivers, toasted	1/4 c. white wine vinegar

In a large bowl, combine potatoes, scallions, celery, parsley, almonds, celery seed, salt and pepper. In another bowl, mix together blue cheese, sour cream and vinegar. Pour over potatoes and toss to coat. Chill overnight. Serves 10 to 12.

What is patriotism but the love of the good things we ate in our childhood?
-Lin Yutang

Roasted Corn with Rosemary Butter

What could be better than fresh sweet corn, roasted in the husk?

6 ears yellow sweet corn, in husks

1/4 c. butter, softened
1 t. fresh rosemary, chopped

Pull back husks on corn, leaving them attached. Rinse corn and remove silk; pat corn dry. In a small bowl, blend together butter and rosemary; brush over corn. Replace husks and roast corn on the grill for about 15 minutes, turning every so often until tender. Serves 6.

*Hats off! Along the street there comes
A blare of bugles, a ruffle of drums,
A flash of color beneath the sky:
Hats off!
The flag is passing by.*
-Henry Holcomb Bennett

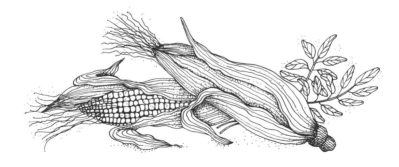

Strawberry Shortcake

For a luscious red, white & blue dessert, mix blueberries with the strawberries.

2 c. biscuit baking mix
2 T. sugar
1/2 c. milk
1/4 c. margarine, melted

1 qt. strawberries,
    hulled and halved
whipped cream

Preheat oven to 450 degrees. Beat biscuit mix, sugar, milk and margarine together until just mixed. Knead 8 to 10 times on a lightly floured surface. Pat dough into a greased 8" cake pan. Bake for 15 to 20 minutes until golden. Let cool slightly, and remove from pan. Split shortcake crosswise and spoon berries in the middle. Replace top half of shortcake and top with whipped cream. Serves 6.

Anchor the 4 corners of your picnic tablecloth with bricks. You can paint the bricks to match the occasion, using them over & over again. For a birthday party, tie the ribbons of helium balloons through the holes in the bricks. Instant celebration!

Minty Iced Tea

*For best tea results, always bring cold water
to a rolling boil.*

8 c. boiling water
8 mint herbal teabags
sugar to taste

8 c. ice cubes
fresh mint sprigs

In a large glass container, pour water over teabags and allow to
steep for 30 minutes. Remove teabags; stir in sugar to taste and
add ice cubes. Pour into glasses full of ice and top each with a
fresh sprig of mint. Serves 12.

California Lemonade

*Cardamom is a fragrant spice from India that tastes
much like cinnamon.*

1-1/2 c. sugar
1 c. lemon juice

5 cardamom seeds, ground

Combine sugar and lemon juice; boil over medium heat for 8 to
10 minutes. Remove from heat and cool. Add cardamom seeds
and chill in refrigerator. To prepare lemonade, mix 4 tablespoons
of concentrate with one quart sparkling water. Makes enough
concentrate for 10 quarts.

All-American Cookout

Red, white and beautiful...

Fabric-Decorated Basket

Turn a plain wicker basket into a beautiful picnic basket!
You'll need:

spray paint
a basket
1/4 yd. fabric with large
    printed design

1" wide paintbrush
découpage sealer
soft cloth
clear acrylic spray

Spray paint basket and let dry completely. Cut out the design from
your fabric and, following instructions on découpage sealer, brush
onto wrong side of fabric. Place fabric over the basket and, using a
warm, damp cloth, press the fabric in place around the body of the
basket. Let dry. Spray basket with acrylic spray and let dry again.
You might try an antique rose-colored fabric on a sage green basket,
or cheery sunflowers on a hunter green basket. Line with a pretty
kitchen towel and fill with goodies.

Sponge-Painted Napkins

Select a solid color cotton fabric for napkins. Cut fabric into
16-inch squares. Wash, dry and press with a warm iron. Sew a
straight stitch all around the edges of the fabric, about 1/2 inch in
from the edge. Fringe the fabric to the stitching. Trace the pattern
you want on your napkins...hearts, squares, diamonds,
stars...onto cardboard. Cut out the cardboard pattern and trace
onto a sponge. Then cut out the sponge all around the pattern
with an artist's blade. Dip the sponge in acrylic paint and stamp
your pattern onto the napkin. After the paint has thoroughly dried,
press with a hot dry iron over a protective piece of cloth to set
the paint.

Apple Candles

You'll need a dozen apples and the same number of tea lights or votive candles, plus a lemon. Cut a thin slice off the bottom of each apple so it will stand upright. Core each apple, widening the space to accommodate a tea light or votive. Sprinkle lemon juice on the apple to keep it from turning brown. Insert candles and light.

Luminarias

Light the way to your next evening celebration with a row of luminarias...beautiful on the beach or lighting a pathway to your late evening outdoor supper. Small brown lunch bags or white bakery bags work perfectly. Use a hole punch to create a design that will let the light shine through. Put sand, kitty litter or gravel in the bottom of the bags to keep them firmly upright. Fill glass votives with candles and place in the bags, anchored by the sand. A charming glow!

For a special effect, use heart or star-shaped hole punches on your luminarias. If it's windy out, weigh the bags down by placing bricks inside.

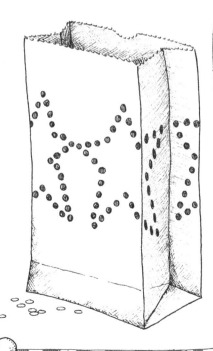

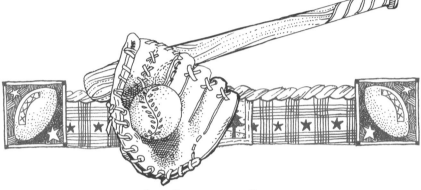

Chunky Gazpacho

Serve in big, icy mugs garnished with stalks of celery.

2-1/2 c. tomato juice
3 T. lemon juice
1/4 c. plus 1 T. olive oil
6 large tomatoes, peeled and
    chopped
2 cucumbers, peeled and
    chopped

1/2 c. green peppers,
    chopped
1/2 c. onion, finely chopped
1 clove garlic, minced
hot pepper sauce to taste
salt and pepper to taste

Whisk together tomato juice, lemon juice and olive oil; set aside. In a large mixing bowl, combine the chopped vegetables; pour dressing over vegetables and mix. Add hot pepper sauce, salt and pepper to taste. Cover and chill; serve cold. Serves 6.

*A truly rich man is one whose
children run into his arms when his
hands are empty.*
-Anonymous

You're the Greatest!

Grilled Steaks with Herb-Mustard Sauce

Who can resist the aroma of steaks on the grill?

2 boneless strip or ribeye
    steaks, 2-1/2" to 3" thick

salt to taste

Herb-Mustard Sauce:

2 cloves garlic, crushed
2 t. water
2 T. Dijon mustard

1 t. dried basil
1/2 t. thyme
1/2 t. pepper

On high power, microwave garlic and water together. Stir in mustard, basil, thyme and pepper; spread onto both sides of steaks. Place steaks on grid over medium ash-covered coals and grill. Grill strip steaks for 8 to 9 minutes per side or ribeyes 6 to 7 minutes per side, depending on thickness, for medium-rare to medium doneness. Season steaks with salt as desired. Carve steaks crosswise into thick slices. Makes 4 servings.

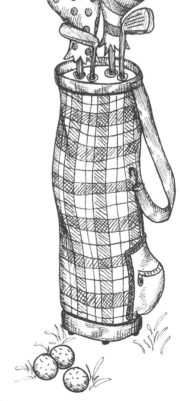

*To have grown
wise and kind
is the greatest
success of all.*
-Anonymous

Pan-Fried Trout

If your celebration includes a fishing trip, fresh trout is the way to go!

1 lb. bacon
2 onions, thinly sliced
1/2 c. cornmeal
1/2 c. all-purpose flour

3/4 T. salt
1 T. pepper
2 fresh trout, cleaned

Fry bacon in a skillet until crisp. Set aside bacon, leaving some drippings in skillet. Add onions and sauté. Mix together cornmeal, flour, salt and pepper. Dredge trout in cornmeal mixture and coat both sides well. Fry trout in hot drippings and onions until very crisp. Garnish with reserved bacon. Serves 2.

Life isn't a matter of milestones, but of moments.
-Rose Fitzgerald Kennedy

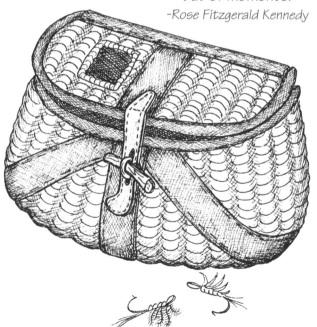

Buttery Roasted Potatoes

If you have a large cast iron skillet, it's the very best pan for roasting potatoes.

2 lbs. Yukon Gold potatoes,
    peeled and cut into
    1" cubes

2 to 4 T. butter, diced
2 t. salt

Preheat oven to 400 degrees. Place potatoes in a large cast iron skillet and add hot water about 1/4 inch deep. Scatter diced butter and salt over potatoes; stir. Bake, uncovered, for about one hour, until potatoes are light golden and water has evaporated. Serves 4 to 6.

Real joy comes not from ease or riches or from the praise of men, but from doing something worthwhile.
-Sir Wilfred Grenfell

Fresh Corn Cakes

Fresh sweet corn is the very taste of summer.

4 ears yellow or white
    sweet corn, husked
1/2 c. cornmeal
1/2 c. all-purpose flour
1 t. salt
1 t. sugar
1/2 t. baking powder

1/4 t. cayenne pepper
1 large egg, beaten
3/4 c. buttermilk
3 T. butter, melted
2 scallions, finely chopped
1 c. sour cream with chives

Cook corn in boiling water for one minute; drain. Cut kernels from the cobs and mash lightly. In a small bowl, combine cornmeal, flour, salt, sugar, baking powder and cayenne pepper. In a separate bowl, whisk egg, buttermilk and butter. Add egg mixture to cornmeal mixture and stir lightly. Stir in scallions and corn. In a heated cast iron skillet that has been coated with oil, place heaping tablespoons of the batter; brown and flip as you would pancakes. Serve sour cream alongside. Makes 4 servings.

*The best and most beautiful things in the world
cannot be seen nor touched...
but are felt in the heart.*
-Helen Keller

You're the greatest! ☆ ☆☆☆

Blackberry-Apple Crunch

This dish tastes delicious after a day of blackberry picking!

2-1/4 c. all-purpose flour,
    divided
2-1/2 c. sugar, divided
1/4 t. salt
1 c. butter, sliced

2-1/2 c. blackberries
4 lbs. Golden Delicious
    apples, cored, peeled
    and thinly sliced
sprinkle of cinnamon

Preheat oven to 350 degrees; grease a 13"x9" baking dish. In medium mixing bowl, combine 2 cups flour, 1-1/2 cups sugar and salt. Cut in butter with pastry blender and mix until crumbly. In another bowl, toss together blackberries, apples, remaining flour and remaining sugar; pour into baking dish. Cover with crumbly topping, sprinkle with cinnamon and bake for about 30 to 45 minutes until fruit bubbles. Cool slightly and serve. Makes 12 to 15 servings.

Chocolate-Peanut Butter Cupcakes

A treat for any celebration!

Filling:

2 T. whipping cream
1/4 c. semi-sweet chocolate
   chips

2 t. sugar
1/4 c. creamy peanut butter

To prepare filling, heat whipping cream in a small saucepan until boiling. Pour cream over chocolate and sugar in a small bowl; stir until combined and chocolate melts. Add peanut butter and mix well. Refrigerate filling for 35 to 40 minutes, until slightly firm.

Cupcakes:

6 T. butter
6-oz. pkg. semi-sweet
   chocolate chips
2 large eggs
2/3 c. sugar

1 t. vanilla extract
3/4 c. all-purpose flour
1/4 t. baking soda
1/4 t. salt

Melt butter and chocolate in a double boiler over low heat; set aside. Beat eggs until foamy. Add sugar and vanilla; beat until fluffy. Beating at low speed, add melted chocolate. Beat in flour, baking soda and salt until just combined. Pour batter into greased muffin tins, filling almost two-thirds full. Roll rounded teaspoonfuls of filling into balls; press one ball lightly into the center of each cupcake. Bake for 15 to 20 minutes at 350 degrees. Makes one dozen.

Fathers' Day Memory Box

Presented on Fathers' Day, this reminder of the past will be a welcome gift.

wooden box
acrylic paint
wood-tone spray finish
craft glue
photocopies of old photographs

decoupage sealer
walnut water-based stain
fine-grain sandpaper
paint brushes
photo mounting corners

Paint box (we used burgundy for a rich color). While it's drying, lightly spray your photocopies with the wood-tone spray. Set them aside to dry, also. When the photocopies are dry, glue photo mounting corners to some of the photocopies. Arrange photos on the box lid in any position you like. Use sealer to glue the photos to the box lid and allow to dry thoroughly. When photocopies are dry, apply the walnut sealer to the entire box, removing any excess with a soft cloth. Allow to dry according to directions. Once dry, apply 2 coats of sealer to the box, allowing each coat to dry before applying the next.

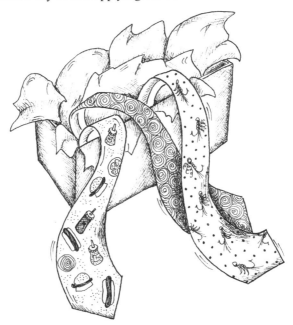

Graduation Cap Gift Box

Choose school colors for the ribbon. A unique gift to fill with money, candy, childhood photos or homemade cookies.

8" round wooden cheese box
tacky glue
craft brush
5/8 yd. satin ribbon

10" square matboard
14" square fabric
decorative tassel
hot glue gun

Using a craft brush, apply glue to the outer rim on the lid of the box. Attach ribbon to the rim. Brush one side of the matboard with glue and place on the wrong side of fabric. Fold in each side of fabric, smoothing out any bumps; let dry thoroughly. Make a small hole in the middle of the board and pull the tassel cord through from the top, using hot glue to attach it to the underside. Fasten the underside of the board to the top of the box lid with hot glue. Center the square on top of the circle to represent a graduation cap.

"Good Luck" Box

If you're sending a high school grad off to college, here's a thoughtful way to say, "We're thinking of you." Gather photos of family members and friends sharing good times together. Collect special mementos…old programs, ticket stubs, newspaper clippings. Select your grad's favorite snack, magazines, stationery and stamps. Put everything in a box. Obtain a map of the grad's destination and use the map to wrap the box.

Join the celebration...

Appetizing Ideas

- Serve peeled and sliced kiwi fruit and honeydew melon on a platter along with thin, rolled-up slices of prosciutto.

- Hollow out a watermelon half and fill with honeydew, cantaloupe and watermelon balls, along with strawberries, blueberries and grapes.

- Mix softened cream cheese with drained, crushed pineapple, chopped pecans, chopped green pepper and salt-free seasoning. Serve with crackers.

- Spread a loaf of party rye bread with mayonnaise. Top with chopped olives, tomato, sweet onion, bacon bits and grated cheese. Broil until bubbly.

- Mix chopped artichoke hearts with grated Parmesan cheese and mayonnaise. Add a bit of chili powder. Spread on mini-bagels and broil until light golden.

- Wrap thin slices of baked ham and Muenster cheese around artichoke hearts, place on top of bread rounds and broil until cheese begins to melt.

- Unwrap an 8-ounce block of cream cheese and pour salsa over the top. Serve with crackers.

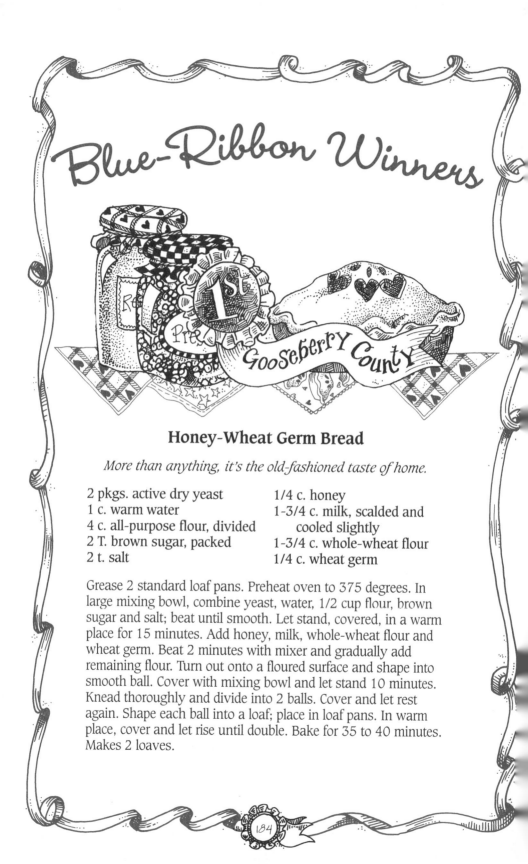

Blue-Ribbon Winners

Honey-Wheat Germ Bread

More than anything, it's the old-fashioned taste of home.

2 pkgs. active dry yeast
1 c. warm water
4 c. all-purpose flour, divided
2 T. brown sugar, packed
2 t. salt

1/4 c. honey
1-3/4 c. milk, scalded and
    cooled slightly
1-3/4 c. whole-wheat flour
1/4 c. wheat germ

Grease 2 standard loaf pans. Preheat oven to 375 degrees. In large mixing bowl, combine yeast, water, 1/2 cup flour, brown sugar and salt; beat until smooth. Let stand, covered, in a warm place for 15 minutes. Add honey, milk, whole-wheat flour and wheat germ. Beat 2 minutes with mixer and gradually add remaining flour. Turn out onto a floured surface and shape into smooth ball. Cover with mixing bowl and let stand 10 minutes. Knead thoroughly and divide into 2 balls. Cover and let rest again. Shape each ball into a loaf; place in loaf pans. In warm place, cover and let rise until double. Bake for 35 to 40 minutes. Makes 2 loaves.

Stuffed Zucchini

*Zucchini are so plentiful, new recipes are always
welcome...especially tasty ones like this.*

1/2 c. bread crumbs
2 T. Parmesan cheese, grated
4 T. butter, divided
1 clove garlic, minced
1/2 c. onion, chopped

1 tomato, peeled and chopped
2 medium zucchini, halved,
   scooped out and pulp
   reserved
salt and pepper to taste

Preheat oven to 350 degrees. In a small dish, toss together
bread crumbs, cheese and 2 tablespoons butter; set aside. Sauté
garlic and onion in remaining butter until soft. Add tomatoes
and zucchini pulp; heat through and mix well. Place zucchini
shells in a greased baking dish; fill with stuffing. Top with bread
crumb mixture; cover and bake for 30 minutes. Season to taste
with salt and pepper and serve right away. Makes 4 servings.

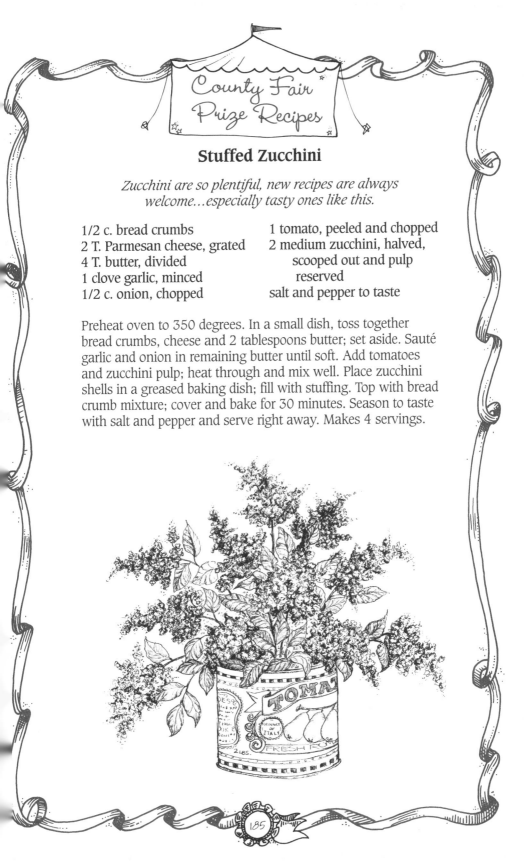

Peachy Cinnamon Jam

The taste of fresh peaches in mid-winter will bring summer back to your breakfast table.

4 c. peaches, finely chopped
2 T. lemon juice
1/2 t. allspice
1/2 t. cinnamon
1/2 t. ground cloves

5-1/2 c. sugar
6 T. liquid pectin
3 1/2-pint canning
   jars and lids,
    sterilized

Toss peaches with lemon juice; combine peaches and spices in a large pot. Bring to a rolling boil; add sugar and boil for one minute. Remove from heat; add pectin. Stir well and skim off foam. Immediately spoon into hot sterilized jars, leaving 1/4-inch headspace. Wipe rims; secure with lids and rings. Process in a boiling water bath for 10 minutes; set jars on a towel to cool. Check for seals. Makes about 3 jars.

Midwest Cornbread

Stone-ground cornmeal gives the bread a really great texture. Have plenty of sweet butter on hand.

1 c. yellow cornmeal
1/4 c. sugar
1 c. all-purpose flour
4 t. baking powder

1/4 c. vegetable oil
2 eggs
1 c. milk

Preheat oven to 425 degrees. Combine cornmeal, sugar, flour and baking powder. Add oil, eggs and milk and beat until smooth. Pour into a greased 9"x9" baking pan; bake for 20 minutes or until golden. Makes 9 to 12 servings.

Fresh Peach Pie

You can use prepared crusts to save time.

2 pie crusts (see recipe this
    chapter)
1 c. sugar
2-1/2 T. cornstarch
1/8 t. salt

1/2 c. water
4 c. peaches, chopped
1/8 t. cinnamon
2 T. butter, sliced

Preheat oven to 425 degrees. Line a 9" glass pie plate with crust. Mix sugar, cornstarch, salt and water; fold in peaches. Pour into pie plate; sprinkle with cinnamon, dot with butter and cover with top crust. Crimp edges of crust to seal; cut several slits in crust. Bake for 10 minutes, then reduce oven to 350 degrees and bake an additional 35 minutes until golden. Serves 6 to 8.

Apple Relish

Delicious served alongside baked ham or pork chops. No need to peel the apples...the peels add eye-pleasing color.

1 large red cooking apple, chopped
1 large green apple, chopped
1/4 c. raisins
1/4 c. ground ginger

1/2 c. onion, chopped
1/4 c. sugar
1/4 c. cider vinegar
1/2 t. salt

In a large saucepan, combine apples, raisins, ginger, onion, sugar, vinegar and salt. Heat until boiling, then reduce heat to low and simmer until onions are tender, about 5 to 7 minutes. Transfer to jars and cover tightly. Let cool to room temperature, then refrigerate. Makes about 3 cups.

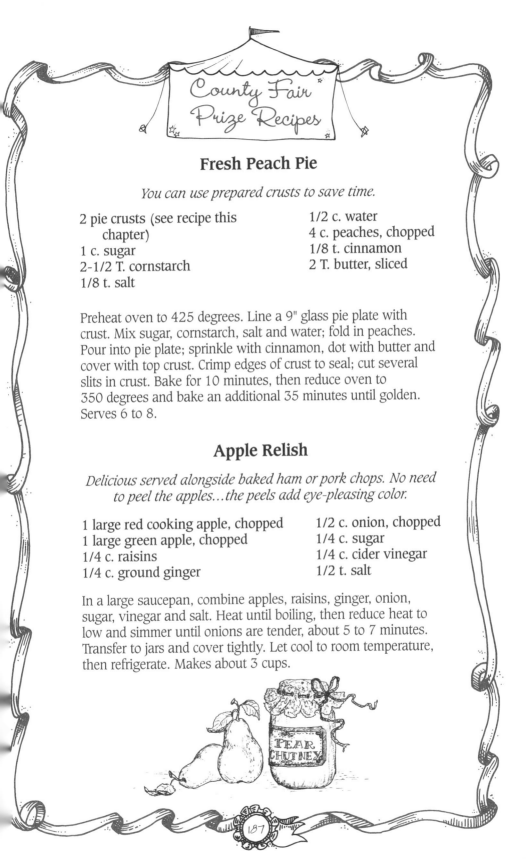

World's Greatest Pie Crust

Make crusts ahead of time and freeze unbaked in pans.
Great to pull out, fill and bake for fresh pie anytime!

1-3/4 c. shortening
5 c. all-purpose flour
1 t. salt

1 egg, slightly beaten
1/4 c. ice water
1 T. vinegar

In mixing bowl, blend shortening, flour and salt with pastry blender until crumbly. Stir in egg, water and vinegar. Divide dough into 5 equal portions and roll out each onto floured surface. Makes 5 crusts.

If you're making a dessert pie, add about
2 teaspoons of sugar to the crust recipe. If you're
making a savory pie, such as chicken pot pie, sprinkle
in some herbs and spices instead.

Prize-Winning Apple Pie

Serve warm à la mode.

2 pie crusts
6 apples, cored and
   chopped
1/2 c. water
2 T. lemon juice
1/2 c. sugar
2 T. all-purpose flour
1-1/2 t. apple pie spice
milk and sugar

Place a pie crust in a 9" pie plate, allowing edges to hang over.
Preheat oven to 375 degrees. Combine apples with water and
lemon juice; set aside. In large mixing bowl, mix sugar, flour
and spice. Drain apples and add to sugar mixture, tossing gently
to coat. Spoon filling into pie plate. Roll out top crust slightly
and cut slits in top (or use pastry-size cookie cutters to create
decorative top.) Place top crust on top of pie and pinch edges
together all the way around joining top and bottom crusts.
Brush top with milk and sprinkle with sugar. Bake for about
30 minutes until crust is golden. Serve 6 to 8.

*Good apple pies are a
considerable part of
our happiness.*
-Jane Austen

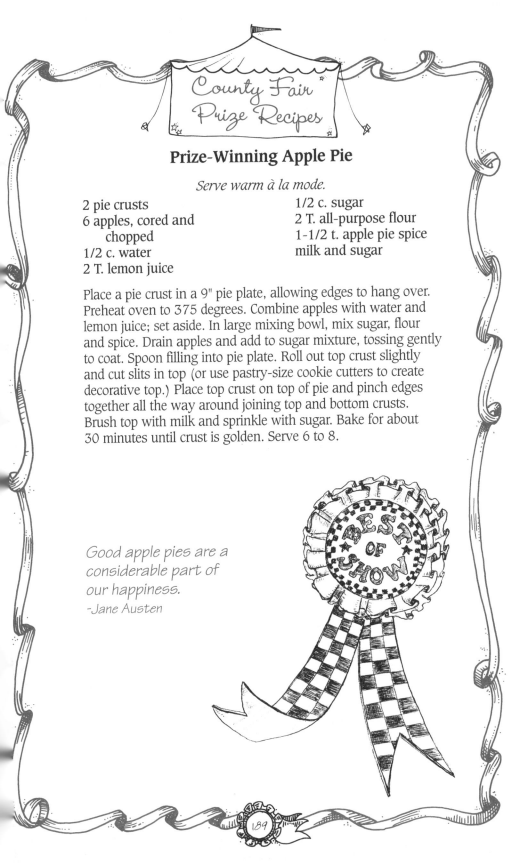

Quick Bread & Butter Pickles

This recipe gets a blue ribbon for homemade taste without the fuss!

32-oz. jar whole kosher
   dill pickles
1-1/2 c. sugar

1 small onion, sliced
2 cinnamon sticks
2 T. vinegar

Drain pickles and cut into chunks 1/2 to one-inch thick; return to jar. Combine sugar, onion, cinnamon sticks and vinegar; pour over pickles. Cover and refrigerate. Stir mixture once a day for 2 to 3 days. Your "homemade" pickles are ready to serve after 3 or 4 days. Makes one quart.

How to pick a prize watermelon? Of course, size is very important! The best melons are firm, symmetrical and heavy for their size and shape. The underside of a watermelon should be yellow. If the melon responds with a hollow thump when you tap it, it's a good sign that it's ripe. Store whole watermelons in the fridge. Cut pieces need to be tightly wrapped.

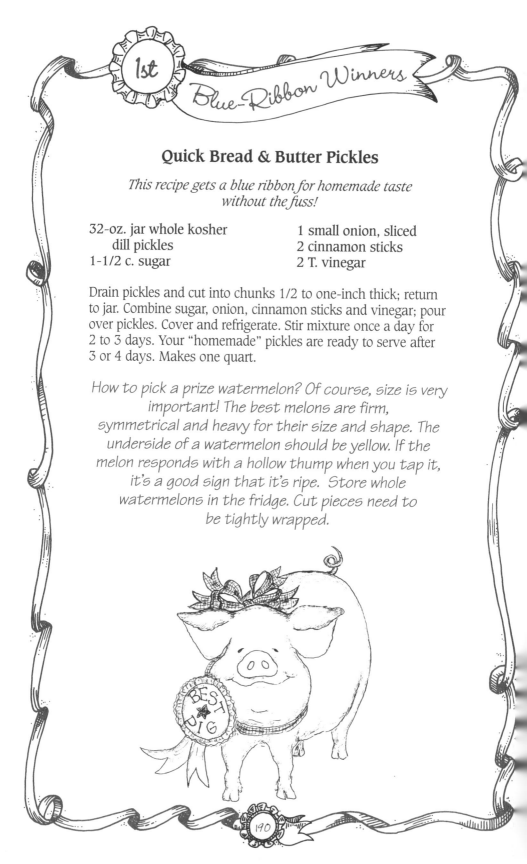

County Fair Chocolate Cake

What's a list of winners without our favorite dessert?

2-1/4 c. all-purpose flour
1/2 t. salt
2 t. baking soda
1/2 c. butter
3 eggs

2-1/4 c. brown sugar, packed
1-1/2 t. vanilla extract
3 sqs. unsweetened
   chocolate, melted
1 c. sour cream
1 c. boiling water

Preheat oven to 375 degrees; grease and flour two, 9" cake pans. Sift flour, salt and baking soda together. In a separate mixing bowl, beat butter until fluffy; add eggs and brown sugar, mixing thoroughly. Add vanilla and chocolate; add sour cream and dry ingredients alternately and beat well. Stir in boiling water. Pour batter into cake pans and bake for 25 minutes, or until tester comes out clean. Frost with Fudge Frosting. Makes 8 to 10 servings.

Fudge Frosting:

1/2 c. butter
4 sqs. unsweetened chocolate
1/2 c. milk

1 lb. powdered sugar
2 t. vanilla extract

In a saucepan over low heat, melt butter and chocolate. Combine milk, sugar and vanilla; add chocolate. Set in a container of ice water and stir until icing thickens.

Try using a plastic knife to cut your next pan of brownies. . . smooth edges all over!

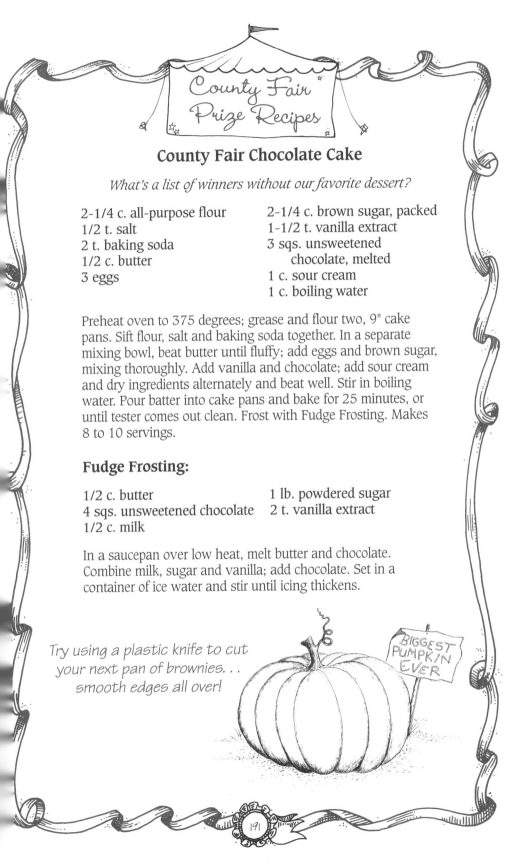

BIGGEST PUMPKIN EVER

Peach Butter

The taste of summer...captured in a jar!

5 lbs. peaches
1/4 c. lemon juice
1/2 c. water
1-1/2 c. sugar

5 to 6 1/2-pint canning
    jars and lids,
    sterilized

Heat a large pot of water to a boil. For easy peeling, score an "X" on both ends of each peach, then drop it into the boiling water for 30 seconds. Transfer peaches to a cold bowl of water. When cool enough to handle, peel, pit and slice the peaches.

Combine peaches, lemon juice and water in a large saucepan. Cook over medium-high heat, stirring often, until the fruit is quite soft, 15 to 20 minutes. Let fruit cool slightly; purée in a food processor to produce about 6-1/2 cups purée. Return the purée to the saucepan and add the sugar. Cook over medium heat, stirring frequently to prevent scorching, until the mixture is thick and creamy, about 25 to 30 minutes.

Stir well; skim off foam. Immediately spoon into hot sterilized jars, leaving 1/4-inch headspace. Wipe rims; secure with lids and rings. Process in a boiling water bath for 10 minutes; set jars on a towel to cool. Check for seals. Makes 5 to 6 jars.

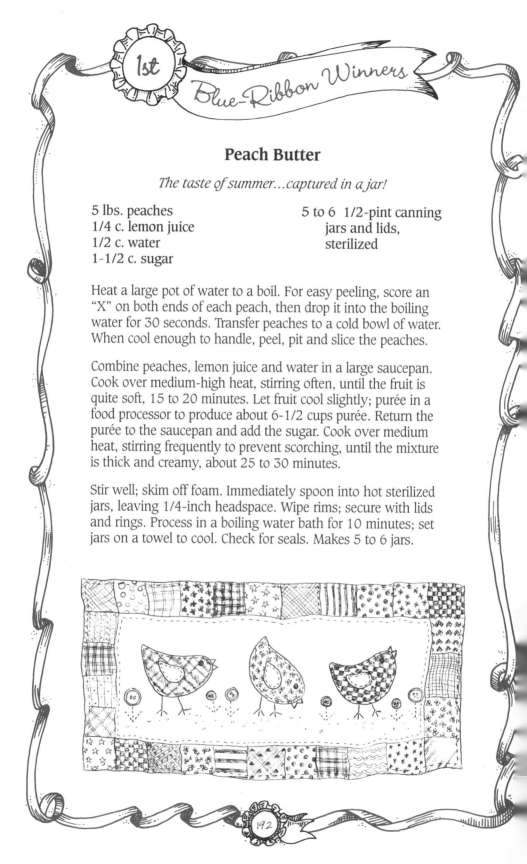

Fair-ly fantastic projects...

Canning Jar Potpourri

These "canned" potpourri collections make beautiful gifts any time of year. Layer the ingredients for a nice effect. Make your own labels and paste on for a true personalized touch. You'll need:

several vintage canning jars
2 T. cinnamon
1 T. ground cloves
mixed, dried mint leaves
sandalwood chips, divided
mixed, dried herb leaves
dried marigold petals, divided
cedar chips or shavings (available at pet stores)
lavender buds
scented oil
dried tea roses, peonies and hydrangeas

Combine cinnamon and cloves and place in the bottom of the jars. Layer scant cupfuls of ingredients in the following order: mint leaves, sandalwood chips, herbs, marigolds, cedar chips, lavender, marigolds, sandalwood chips and oil. Complete the jars by adding dried flowers, petals and more oil before placing lid on jars. To use, leave jar open or put a scrap of netting or fabric over the opening, secured with a canning jar ring.

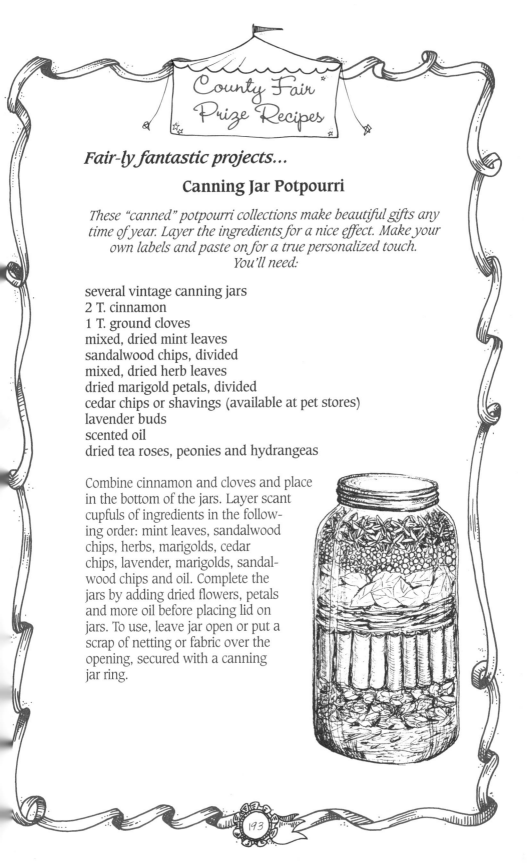

Old-Fashioned Ice Cream Social

Fresh Peach Ice Cream

This creamy recipe tastes very rich...brings back memories of summer on the farm. Garnish with fresh mint.

5 c. milk, divided
4 egg yolks
8 peaches, peeled, pitted and
    mashed
2 T. lemon juice

2-1/2 T. vanilla extract
1/2 t. ground ginger
1/2 t. almond extract
2 14-oz. cans sweetened
    condensed milk

Combine 2-1/2 cups of the milk and the egg yolks in a heavy saucepan and whisk well. Cook and stir over medium heat about 10 minutes, or until mixture will coat a spoon. (Do not overcook, or it will turn into scrambled eggs!) Combine egg mixture with remaining milk, peaches and all remaining ingredients in a large bowl and stir well. Cover and chill. Pour mixture into the freezer section of an ice cream freezer. Freeze according to manufacturer's directions. Spoon into a container with a tight-fitting lid and freeze for an hour, or until completely firm. Serves 12 to 24, depending on serving size.

I scream, you scream, we all scream for ice cream!
-Children's rhyme

Orange-Filled Napoleons

Easy to make and elegant to serve!

8-oz. pkg. frozen puff pastry
   sheets, thawed
2 c. vanilla ice cream,
   softened

1 navel orange, peeled and
    thinly sliced
powdered sugar

Preheat oven to 375 degrees. Unfold pastry and cut into
8 rectangles. Place on an ungreased baking sheet; bake for
20 minutes or until pastries are puffed and golden. Cool on wire
rack. To serve, split pastries lengthwise. Spoon ice cream onto
one half; top with orange slices and replace pastry top. Dust
with powdered sugar and serve immediately. Serves 8.

A swarm of bees in May
Is worth a load of hay;
A swarm of bees in June
Is worth a silver spoon;
A swarm of bees in July
Is not worth a fly.
-Old English proverb

Old-Fashioned Ice Cream Social

Easy Strawberry Ice Cream

Garnish with a ripe red strawberry and a wafer cookie. Vary the recipe with different fruits throughout the summer.

2/3 c. very cold buttermilk
1 t. orange extract

2 10-oz. pkgs. frozen
   strawberries, slightly
   thawed

Place buttermilk and orange extract into a blender or food processor. Cut slightly thawed fruit into chunks and add to blender. Whirl until mixture is smooth and ice cream consistency. Serve immediately. Makes about 4-1/2 cups.

Bake a batch of your favorite cookies...chocolate chip, peanut butter, oatmeal, sugar...and sandwich different flavors of ice cream inside. Yum!

Creamy Orange Pops

*Pure orange juice makes these taste so much
better than store-bought.*

1 pt. vanilla ice cream,
   softened
6-oz. can frozen orange juice
   concentrate, thawed

1/4 c. honey
1-1/2 c. milk
12 5-oz. paper drinking cups
12 wooden treat sticks

In large bowl, mix together ice cream, orange juice concentrate
and honey. Gradually beat in milk. Freeze in small wax paper
cups or ice cube tray. Insert sticks into paper cup molds when
partially frozen. Makes 12.

Raspberry Pops

*Try making these pops with blackberries or strawberries
for a nice variety!*

1/4 c. honey
8-oz. pkg. cream cheese,
   softened
10-oz. pkg. frozen rasp-
   berries, slightly thawed

1 c. bananas, sliced
1 c. heavy cream, whipped
2 c. miniature marshmallows
10 5-oz. paper drinking cups
10 wooden treat sticks

Gradually add honey to cream cheese, mixing until well
blended. Stir in fruit; fold in whipped cream and marshmallows.
Pour into paper cups; insert wooden sticks in center and freeze
until firm. Makes 10 pops.

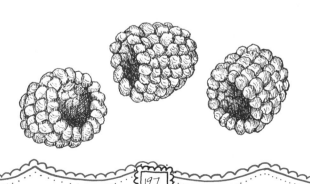

Wild Blueberry Ice

We're using frozen blueberries for ease of preparation...you can use fresh blueberries that you've simmered and stirred in a small amount of water and allowed to cool.

1/4 c. sugar
1/2 c. water

15-oz. pkg. frozen
   blueberries, thawed
   and syrup reserved

In a small saucepan, cook sugar and water over low heat until sugar dissolves. Remove from heat; add syrup from blueberries and half of the berries. Chill thoroughly; pour into an ice cream maker and process according to manufacturer's directions. Serve right away, topped with remaining blueberries. Makes 4 to 6 servings.

Make an ice cream "watermelon"...line a big bowl with softened pistachio ice cream (this will be the rind), and set aside in freezer. Fold chocolate chips (for the seeds) into softened strawberry ice cream. Spoon the strawberry ice cream into the bowl over the pistachio layer. Place bowl in the freezer. To serve, just remove ice cream from bowl and slice into watermelon-shaped wedges.

Honeydew Sorbet

You can also make this recipe with cantaloupe. Delicious!

2 lbs. honeydew melon,
   peeled and seeded
1/2 c. sugar

1/2 c. sweet dessert wine or
   white grape juice
1/4 t. cinnamon

Cut melon into large pieces and purée in blender. Add sugar, wine or juice and cinnamon; blend until sugar dissolves. Pour mixture into an ice cream maker; process according to manufacturer's directions. Freeze in a tightly-covered container. Makes about 3 cups.

Coffee Sherbet

Try this recipe with a variety of flavored coffees like vanilla, almond, hazelnut...mmm!

2/3 c. sugar
4 c. strong, hot brewed coffee
1/2 c. milk

Combine sugar and hot coffee until sugar dissolves. Add milk and chill thoroughly. Freeze in an ice cream maker according to manufacturer's instructions, and serve immediately. Makes about 5 cups.

The only emperor is the emperor of ice cream.
-Wallace Stevens

Apricot Sundaes

Your favorite vanilla ice cream serves as a base for this delicious fruity sundae.

12-oz. jar apricot preserves
1-1/2 t. lemon zest
1/3 c. pineapple juice

1/3 c. brown sugar,
packed
vanilla ice cream

Combine all ingredients in bowl except ice cream; microwave on high for 2 minutes. Stir until sugar is dissolved and serve warm over ice cream. Makes 2 cups topping.

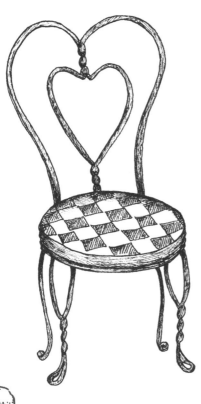

My advice to you is not to inquire why...but just enjoy your ice cream while it's on your plate. That's my philosophy.
-Thornton Wilder

Coffee Cream Parfaits

Sprinkle chocolate curls on top for an extra treat!

1 qt. vanilla ice cream,
   softened
1 c. coffee liqueur
1/2 c. heavy cream

1-1/2 t. sugar
1-1/2 t. instant espresso
   powder

In tall ice cream or parfait glasses, layer ice cream and liqueur. Chill in freezer for half an hour or more. When ready to serve, whip together cream, sugar and espresso until soft peaks form; top parfaits. Serves 4.

Deluxe Ice Cream Sandwiches

Cool vanilla ice cream sandwiched between chewy, thin oatmeal cookies...yummy!

1-1/2 c. butter
3 c. rolled oats, uncooked
1-1/2 T. all-purpose flour
1 t. salt
1-3/4 c. sugar

2 t. vanilla extract
2 eggs, lightly beaten
1/2 gal. vanilla ice cream
Garnish: sprinkles

Melt butter in a large saucepan over low heat. Let cool; add oats, flour, salt, sugar and vanilla. Stir well to combine; add eggs and mix thoroughly. Cover baking sheets with parchment paper; butter paper. Spoon 1-1/2 tablespoons of dough for each cookie onto baking sheets 3 inches apart, making 24. Flatten dough into circles. Bake at 375 degrees until golden, 12 to 14 minutes. Let cool. Unwrap a square block of ice cream and slice into one-inch thick slices, cutting into squares big enough to slightly overlap edges of cookies. Sandwich ice cream between cookies. Dip edges of sandwiches into sprinkles. Wrap individually and freeze until ready to serve. Makes one dozen.

Classic Chocolate Shake

*Brings back the days of ice cream parlors and
dime-store counters.*

1-1/2 c. sugar
1 c. water
1/2 c. unsweetened baking
   cocoa

1 t. vanilla extract
4 T. milk
1-1/2 qts. vanilla
   ice cream

Combine sugar and water in a heavy saucepan; stir over
medium-low heat until sugar is completely dissolved. Increase
heat and bring to a boil. Place cocoa in a bowl and gradually
whisk in sugar syrup. Return mixture to saucepan and boil one
minute, continuing to whisk. Whisk in vanilla, pour into bowl
immediately and allow to cool completely. Chill, covered, at least
one hour. For each milkshake, pour 3 tablespoons syrup and
one tablespoon milk into a blender. Add 1-1/2 cups ice cream
and blend until smooth. Pour into a tall glass and serve with a
big paper straw. Serves 4.

*We dare not trust our wit for making our
house pleasant to our friend, so we buy
ice cream.*
-Ralph Waldo Emerson

Fresh Fruit Ices

Make a variety of cool, refreshing ices with just a few ingredients!

1 env. unflavored gelatin
1/2 c. cold water
1 c. fruit juice of your
    choice...orange, cherry
    grapefruit, cranberry,
    strawberry, apple

6 T. lemon juice
4 T. sugar
1 c. sliced fruit...peaches,
    strawberries, melon
Garnish: superfine sugar,
    lemon or lime wedges

Combine gelatin and water in a saucepan over low heat; stir until gelatin is completely dissolved. Stir in juice, sugar and fruit. Pour into a bowl; place in the freezer until almost set. With an electric mixer, beat on high speed until light and fluffy. Cover and return to freezer to set. For an extra treat, chill glasses in the freezer. When ready to serve, run a wedge of lemon or lime around the rims of glasses and dip rims into superfine sugar, then fill with fruit ice. Garnish with a citrus wedge. Serves 8.

In the morning, very early,
That's the time I love to go
Barefoot where the fern grows curly
And grass is cool between each toe,
On a summer morning-O!
On a summer morning.
    -Rachel Field

Tantalizing toppings...

Chocolate-Peanut Butter Sauce

2 sqs. semi-sweet chocolate, chopped
14-oz. can sweetened condensed milk

2 T. creamy peanut butter
2 T. milk
1 t. vanilla extract

Melt together all ingredients except vanilla in a medium saucepan over low heat, stirring constantly. Remove from heat; stir in vanilla. Serve warm; store in the refrigerator. Makes about 1-1/2 cups.

Blueberry Syrup

1 c. blueberries
1/2 c. sugar
1/4 vanilla bean, split lengthwise

3/4 c. water
2-1/2 T. lemon juice

Combine berries, sugar and vanilla bean in a medium saucepan. Add water and bring to a boil over medium-high heat. Reduce heat to low and simmer about 5 minutes. Remove vanilla bean and pour mixture into a blender. Add lemon juice and blend until smooth. Makes about 2 cups.

Strawberry Preserves

Serve over vanilla ice cream, or swirl into whipped cream for a strawberry "fool."

4 qts. strawberries, hulled   juice of 1 lemon
9 c. sugar

Layer strawberries with sugar in a glass bowl. Cover and let stand overnight. Pour strawberry mixture into a deep, non-aluminum saucepan. Add lemon juice; bring to a boil. Let simmer 5 minutes. Return strawberry mixture to bowl; cover and let stand 24 hours. Return strawberry mixture to pan; bring to a rapid boil until syrup has thickened, about 30 minutes. Cool slightly; spoon into hot sterilized 1/2-pint jars, leaving 1/4-inch headspace. Wipe rims; secure with lids and rings. Process in a boiling water bath for 10 minutes; set jars on a towel to cool. Check for seals. Or pack into freezer containers and freeze up to several months. The preserves can be refrigerated for several weeks, if you don't intend to freeze them.

More Quick Topping Ideas

Crushed chocolate sandwich cookies
Peanuts, cashews or macadamia nuts
Colored sugar sprinkles
Chocolate sprinkles
Crushed hard candies
Sweetened cocoa powder (fill a big shaker full)
Chocolate chips and chunks
Butterscotch chips
Whipped topping, tinted with a few drops of food coloring
     just for fun
Fresh blueberries, strawberries, raspberries or blackberries
Crushed pineapple
Honey
…and don't forget the maraschino cherries!

Tex-Mex Feast

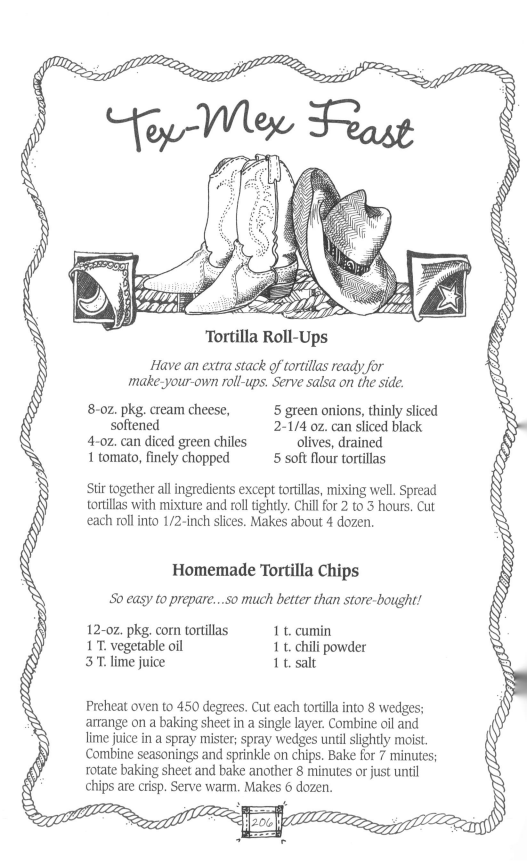

Tortilla Roll-Ups

*Have an extra stack of tortillas ready for
make-your-own roll-ups. Serve salsa on the side.*

8-oz. pkg. cream cheese,
   softened
4-oz. can diced green chiles
1 tomato, finely chopped

5 green onions, thinly sliced
2-1/4 oz. can sliced black
   olives, drained
5 soft flour tortillas

Stir together all ingredients except tortillas, mixing well. Spread
tortillas with mixture and roll tightly. Chill for 2 to 3 hours. Cut
each roll into 1/2-inch slices. Makes about 4 dozen.

Homemade Tortilla Chips

So easy to prepare...so much better than store-bought!

12-oz. pkg. corn tortillas
1 T. vegetable oil
3 T. lime juice

1 t. cumin
1 t. chili powder
1 t. salt

Preheat oven to 450 degrees. Cut each tortilla into 8 wedges;
arrange on a baking sheet in a single layer. Combine oil and
lime juice in a spray mister; spray wedges until slightly moist.
Combine seasonings and sprinkle on chips. Bake for 7 minutes;
rotate baking sheet and bake another 8 minutes or just until
chips are crisp. Serve warm. Makes 6 dozen.

Nachos Magnifico

Vary the ingredients according to your creativity and taste.

1 lb. ground beef
1 c. onion, chopped
salt and pepper to taste
2 15-oz. cans refried beans
4-oz. can diced green chiles
1 to 2 c. salsa
1 c. cheddar cheese,
   shredded
1 c. mozzarella cheese,
   shredded

1 c. Monterey Jack cheese,
   shredded
6-oz. container guacamole
2-1/4 oz. can sliced black
   olives, drained
1 c. green onion, chopped
1-1/2 c. sour cream
tortilla chips

Heat oven to 400 degrees; lightly spray a 13"x9" baking dish
with cooking spray. In a skillet, brown ground beef and onion;
drain. Add salt and pepper. Spread refried beans in bottom of
baking dish and cover with beef. Layer on chiles and salsa.
Sprinkle with cheeses; cover and bake for 35 to 40 minutes.
Top with guacamole, olives, green onion and sour cream.
Serve right away with warm, crisp tortilla chips. Makes 6 to
8 servings.

*...to get the full value of
a joy, you must have
somebody
to divide it with.*
-Mark Twain

Chile Con Queso Dip

Serve with tortilla chips, crisp cold veggies and baked pita wedges.

28-oz. can plum tomatoes, drained and chopped
2 4-oz. cans diced green chiles, drained

1 c. whipping cream
1 lb. Cheddar cheese, shredded
salt and pepper to taste

Simmer tomatoes and chiles in a saucepan over low heat for about 15 minutes. Stirring constantly, add cream and cheese and continue cooking until mixture thickens. Season with salt and pepper and serve warm. Makes about 8 cups.

Wealth I ask not, hope nor love,
Nor a friend to know me;
All I ask, the heaven above
And the road below me.
-Robert Louis Stevenson

Tortilla Soup

For a heartier soup, add cubed chicken breasts.

6 14-1/2 oz. cans chicken
   broth
2 4-oz. cans diced mild
   green chiles, drained
2 cloves garlic, minced
1/3 c. fresh mint, chopped
1 t. chili powder
1 t. cumin
red pepper flakes to taste

1 c. tomatoes, chopped
2 avocados, pitted, peeled
   and chopped
4 slices bacon, cooked
   and crumbled
1/2 c. plus 2 T. fresh cilantro,
   chopped and divided
tortilla chips, slightly crushed
Garnish: sour cream

In a large stockpot, combine chicken broth, chiles and seasonings; bring to a boil. Reduce heat to low and simmer for about one hour. While soup is simmering, combine tomatoes, avocados, bacon and 1/2 cup cilantro in a bowl. To serve, ladle broth into individual soup bowls, place a scoopful of tomato mixture on each and and top with tortilla chips. Garnish with sour cream and remaining cilantro and serve right away. Serves 12.

Bright bandanas make colorful napkins for any barbecue. Tie one around each person's set of utensils. After the party, just toss them in the wash.

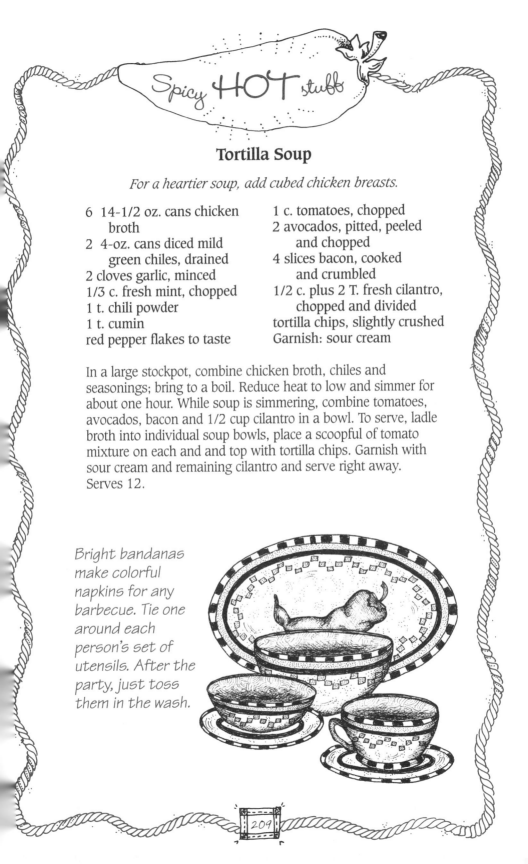

Texas Border Barbecued Beef Ribs

Make the chile sauce the night before to allow the flavors to ripen. Serve extra sauce at the table.

1/3 c. Red Chile Sauce	1 small yellow onion, diced
1 c. dry red wine	1/2 t. salt
2 T. olive oil	pepper to taste
1 large clove garlic, minced	4 lbs. beef short ribs

Combine all ingredients except ribs in a bowl; let stand for 15 to 30 minutes so flavors can blend. Arrange ribs on a large roasting pan in a single layer. Brush marinade over ribs, covering completely; rub into ribs. Position grill rack 3 inches above coals. Remove ribs from marinade; reserve marinade in a separate bowl. Place ribs directly on the heated grill; sear for 10 minutes on each side. Remove ribs; raise rack another 2 inches. Cover rack with foil; use a fork to poke several holes in the foil for ventilation. Place ribs on the foil and brush with remaining marinade. Grill ribs for about 40 minutes, turning every 5 minutes and basting often, until crusty and brown. Serves 4.

Red Chile Sauce:

2 t. shortening	2 c. beef broth
2 T. all-purpose flour	1 clove garlic, minced
1/4 c. mild red chile pepper, ground	1/4 t. dried cilantro
	1/4 t. cumin

Melt shortening in a large saucepan over medium heat. Gradually add flour, stirring with a fork to mix thoroughly until flour turns golden. Remove pan from heat; stir in chile pepper, then broth. Add remaining ingredients; return pan to heat. Simmer, uncovered, for 30 to 45 minutes. Adjust seasonings if necessary. Allow to cool; refrigerate overnight. Makes 2 cups.

Broiled Chicken Breasts with Lime

Serve with a garnish of avocado and lime slices.

2 T. honey
3 T. lime juice
2 T. lime zest
1/2 t. cumin

1/3 c. tequila or lime juice
4 boneless, skinless chicken
  breasts

Preheat broiler and position rack about 4 inches below broiler. In a medium bowl, whisk together honey, lime juice, lime zest, cumin and tequila or lime juice. Dredge chicken breasts in mixture to coat thoroughly. Broil for 6 to 8 minutes, basting several times and turning once, until juices run clear when pierced. Serves 4.

Fresh Lime

Can't grill outside due to weather? Use your oven broiler, waiting until the last few minutes of cooking to baste meat and veggies.

Spicy Grilled Vegetables

Place directly on the grill for true smoky flavor.

4 medium potatoes, sliced
    diagonally
3 large carrots, sliced
    lengthwise
2 large zucchini, sliced
    crosswise

2 T. onion, chopped
1 T. lime juice
1/3 c. olive oil
1/2 t. cumin
1/2 t. salt
1/4 t. pepper

Place potatoes and carrots in a medium saucepan and cover with water. Boil for 10 minutes over high heat. Drain and place in a large bowl; add zucchini slices. Combine remaining ingredients in a small bowl. Pour over vegetables, tossing to coat well. Let stand for about 15 minutes, allowing flavors to blend. Grill vegetables for about 3 minutes on each side, turning once. Serve hot. Makes 4 to 6 servings.

For a treat, let the kids pitch a tent in the backyard and sleep under the stars.

Fresh Corn-Tomato Salsa

A delicious, spicy chip dip...or spoon on top of Spanish rice.

1 c. fresh corn, cooked
1 large tomato, peeled,
   seeded and chopped
1 small cucumber, peeled
   and chopped
1 small onion, finely chopped

1 stalk celery, chopped
1 jalapeño pepper, chopped
1 large garlic clove, minced
3 T. lime juice
1/2 t. cumin
1/2 t. salt

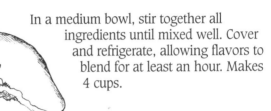

In a medium bowl, stir together all ingredients until mixed well. Cover and refrigerate, allowing flavors to blend for at least an hour. Makes 4 cups.

Papaya Salsa

Tasty salsa that can be prepared up to 3 days ahead of your party. Serve with chicken fajitas or blue corn chips.

1 medium papaya, diced
1 small red pepper, diced
1 small red onion, thinly
   sliced
1 jalapeño pepper, diced

1 clove garlic, minced
6 T. lime juice
1/4 c. pineapple juice
1/4 c. fresh cilantro, chopped
salt and pepper to taste

Combine all ingredients well and chill, allowing flavors to blend. Makes 2 to 3 cups.

"Salsa" is simply sauce! You can make a variety of salsas with a combination of sweet fruit and hot peppers. Experiment with watermelon, peaches or nectarines.

Peanut Butter Round-Up Cookies

A favorite snack for cowboys and cowgirls. You can use creamy or crunchy peanut butter, depending on preference.

2 c. shortening
2 c. brown sugar, packed
1-1/2 c. sugar
4 eggs
2 c. peanut butter

4 c. all-purpose flour
4 t. baking soda
1 t. salt
2 c. rolled oats, uncooked

Preheat oven to 350 degrees. Beat shortening and sugars together until creamy. Add eggs and peanut butter; beat well. Sift together flour, baking soda and salt. Add to shortening mixture, blending well. Stir in oats. Shape dough into one-inch balls. Place onto ungreased baking sheets; make a criss-cross design with a fork on each cookie. Bake for 8 to 10 minutes. Makes 6 dozen.

Iced Cowboy Coffee

For iced coffee, make a trayful of coffee ice cubes. This recipe is also outstanding served warm, garnished with a heaping scoop of ice cream.

5 c. milk
2 T. instant coffee powder
1 whole nutmeg, finely
    grated

1 sq. milk chocolate, grated
2 T. brown sugar, packed
Optional: 6 T. brandy

In a medium saucepan, whisk together milk, coffee, nutmeg, chocolate and sugar until heated through. When the chocolate has melted, add the brandy, if using, and mix thoroughly. Serve over ice. Makes 4 to 6 servings.

Lone Star Pecan Cake

So rich, it needs no frosting. Dust with powdered sugar over a star stencil, just for fun.

1 lb. butter, softened
2 c. sugar
6 eggs, beaten
1 t. lemon extract

4 c. all-purpose flour
1-1/2 t. baking powder
4 c. pecan halves
2 c. golden raisins

Grease and flour a 9" tube pan; preheat oven to 300 degrees. Blend butter and sugar in a large mixing bowl; beat until light and fluffy. Gradually add eggs and extract, continuing to beat. Sift flour and baking powder together; add nuts and raisins to the dry mixture. Gradually stir dry ingredients into creamed mixture; blend well. Pour into the prepared pan and bake for 1-1/2 to 2 hours, or until a toothpick comes out clean. Cool for 15 minutes, then remove from pan. Serves 8.

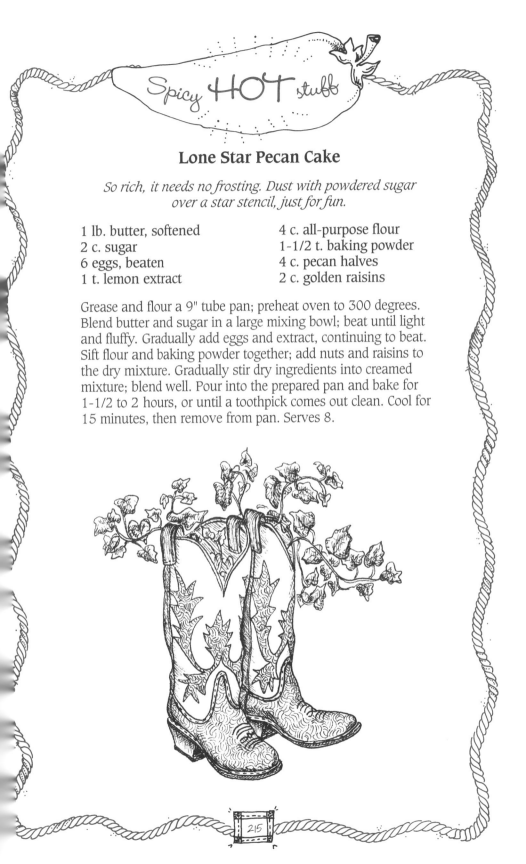

Tex-Mex Feast

Best of the West...

Homemade Invitations

Make your own Tex-Mex party invitations. Purchase blank notes and envelopes, and cut them into simple western shapes like hats, boots, horses, cows or cacti. Use cork stamps to decorate your invitations. Draw a design on the wide end of a cork...a star, heart, chile pepper or boot. Using a sharp knife, cut away the cork from the area outside the pattern, paring about 1/4-inch deep. Press the cork onto a stamp pad and press the design onto your invitations and envelopes. Use markers and gold glitter ("gold dust") to finish off your designs.

Weathered Clay Pot Planters

These planters are so easy, and look great potted with a variety of cactus plants, Mexican heather or herbs. Just rub the outside of new clay pots with buttermilk. Let them stand for 3 weeks in a damp, shaded area like a garage or basement. They'll look like they've been around since the pioneers settled the Old West.

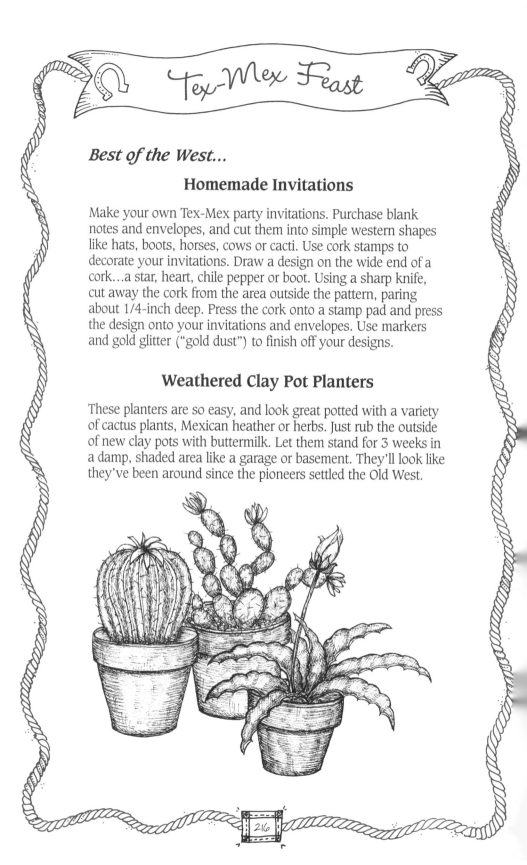

Southwest Chile Garland

A fun decoration with true southwestern flair. You'll need a large-eyed needle, such as a tapestry needle, 36 inches of strong thread or fishing line and 50 whole cayenne peppers. It's a good idea to wear disposable surgical gloves (available at drug stores) when working with the peppers, as they can burn. Never touch a pepper, then touch your eye with your hand. It will burn! Thread the needle and tie a loop at one end. Run the needle through the peppers just below the stem and slide to the end of the string. Repeat until you've reached the desired length. Remove the needle and tie a knot in the thread. Arrange peppers so they face in alternating directions. Hang vertically like the traditional southwestern "ristra." Fresh chiles will dry as they hang.

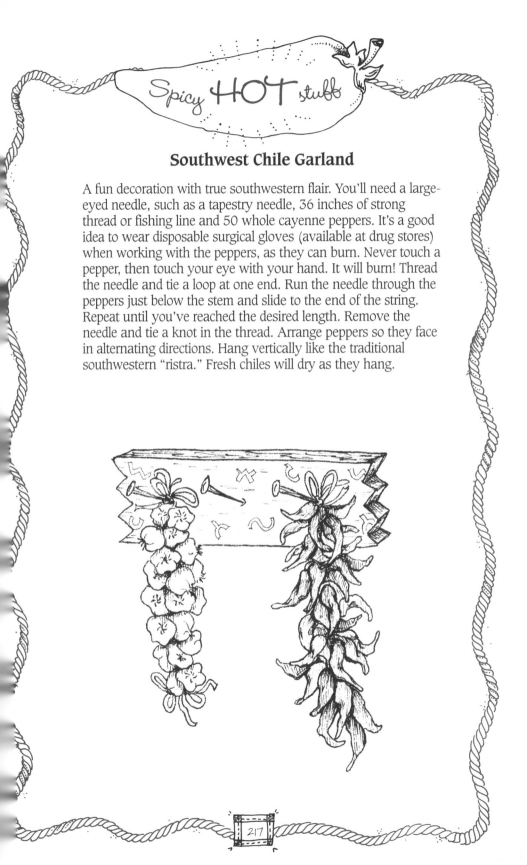

Summer party pointers...

Lighting Ideas

Lighting is extremely important to the atmosphere of any party. Most parties need 2 types of lighting...one to light the scenery and the other to add glow to tables and other eating areas. You can achieve a party mood with bamboo torches, paper lanterns, luminarias (votive candles nestled in sand inside open paper bags), strings of colored lights or tiny white lights. For table lighting, use votive candles tucked inside colored beverage glasses, jelly jars or little clay pots. Taper candles work well inside hurricane shades, and pillar candles can be placed inside crocks, buckets and big clay pots. For even more sparkle, string tiny white lights along your buffet table.

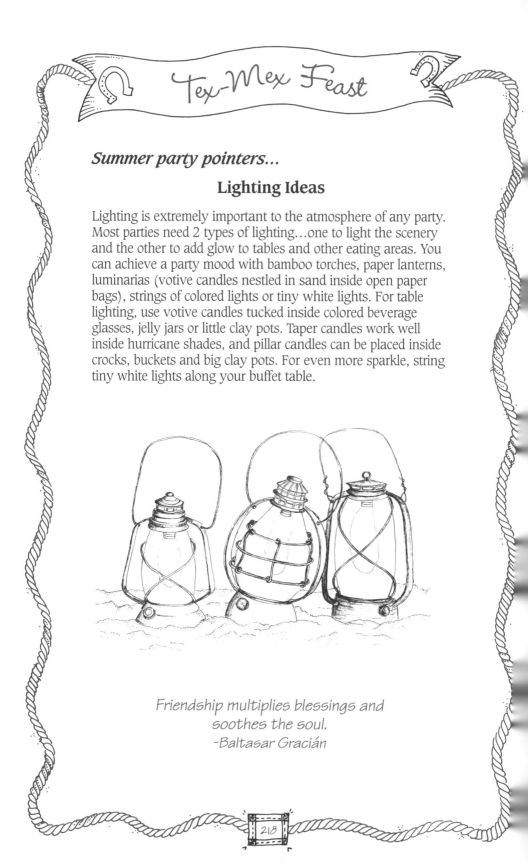

Friendship multiplies blessings and
soothes the soul.
-Baltasar Gracián

Party Piñata

Kids love to take a whack at a real piñata…a papier-maché donkey that's long been a Mexican party tradition. Remember to start early, as the papier-maché will take several days to dry.

1/3 c. all-purpose flour
1/4 c. water
plastic bag
large bowl
large balloon

old newspapers
4 empty tissue tubes
bright-colored poster paint
candies, gum, small toys, trinkets

Mix flour and water; place in a plastic bag and knead until it forms a paste. Put paste in a large bowl and set aside. Blow up balloon. Dip newspaper strips into the paste and cover the balloon to make the body. While that is drying, roll newspaper into a tight ball to make the head and tape it to the body. Cover the head with newspaper strips dipped in paste. To make legs, tape the cardboard tubes to the body and wrap in newspaper strips dipped in paste. Let the piñata dry for 2 days. Paint the body in any combination of colors and designs; add a mouth and eyes. Once the paint has dried, carefully cut a hand-sized hole in the top of the body and fill with candy, gum, small toys and trinkets. Hang the piñata from a tree branch with string. Let the kids take turns hitting the piñata with a large stick or a baseball bat until it breaks, releasing the toys. What fun!

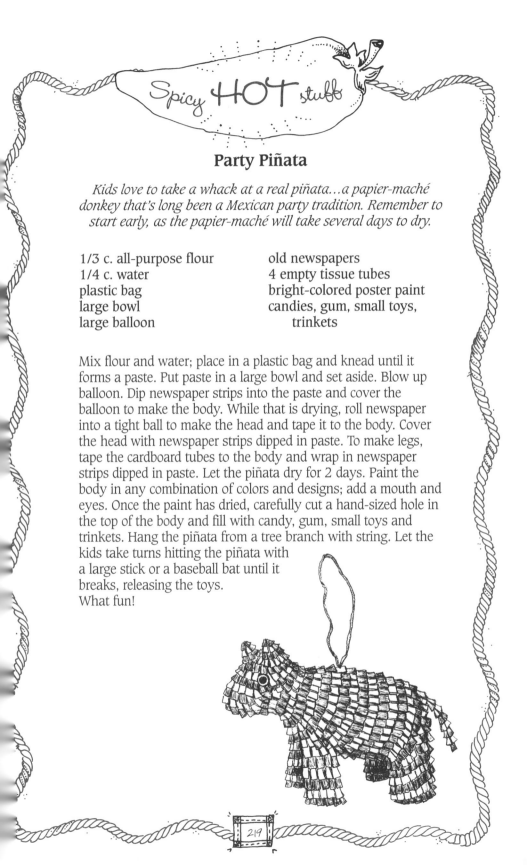

Index

Appetizers

4-Cheese & Peppers Pizza, 82
Artichoke-Red Pepper Dip, 153
Artichoke-Cheese Squares, 117
Blue Cheese Cut-Out Crackers, 132
Broiled Oysters, 98
Championship Artichoke Dip, 14
Cheese-Walnut Grape Rounds, 133
Chile Con Queso Dip, 208
Crunchy Baked Pita Chips, 7
Fresh Veggie Pizza, 6
Goblin Cheese Balls, 20
Homemade Tortilla Chips, 206
Hot Jalapeño Poppers, 56
Marinated Olives, 52
Mushroom Turnovers, 116
Nachos Magnifico, 207
Patchwork Wheel of Brie, 80
Pimento Deviled Eggs, 79
Running Back Popcorn & Peanuts, 13
Smoked Salmon Canapés, 78
Smoked Salmon Cones with
  Horseradish Cream, 130
Soft Pretzels with Mustard, 12
Spicy Black Bean Salsa, 7
Spicy Cheese Tidbits, 17
Tortilla Roll-Ups, 206

Beverages

Almond Tea, 148
Blushing Pink Punch Bowl, 135
California Lemonade, 171
Christmas Wassail, 69
Cinnamon Hot Chocolate, 55
Classic Chocolate Shake, 202
Cranberry Hot Toddies, 54
Creamy Raspberry Smoothie, 157
Iced Cowboy Coffee, 214
Jack Frost Warm-Up, 55
Minty Iced Tea, 171
Old-Fashioned Eggnog, 69
Spiced Apple Cider, 9
Sunrise Punch, 73
Vanilla Coffee, 72
Witch's Brew, 23

Breads

3-Grain Amish Bread, 36
Caraway Rye Bread, 39
Cheddar Cheese Spoon Bread, 37
Crusty Cornmeal Rolls, 38
Frightfully Good Apple-Cheddar
  Bread, 21
Honey-Wheat Germ Bread, 184
Irish Soda Bread, 109
Little Bread Cups, 40
Midwest Cornbread, 186
Orange Muffins, 145
Pumpkin Nut Bread, 76
Ripe Olive Bread, 40
Tomato Bruschetta, 152
Warm Sweet Potato Muffins, 59

Breakfast

Country Quiche, 134
Christmas Casserole, 73
Easy Red Potato Frittata, 143
Herb Omelet, 144
Monte Cristos, 84

Desserts

Apple Kugel, 83
Apricot Sundaes, 200
Blackberry-Apple Crunch, 179
Blackberry-Peach Crisp, 124
Buckeye Candy, 17
Candied Oranges, 67
Cheesecake Bar Cookies, 159
Chocolate Bavarian Cream, 92
Chocolate Cookie Balls, 91

Index

Chocolate Mint Brownies, 58
Chocolate Mousse, 88
Chocolate Orange Cake, 89
Chocolate Puffs, 102
Chocolate-Peanut Butter Cupcakes, 180
Chocolate-Peanut Butter Sauce, 204
Coffee Cream Parfaits, 201
Coffee Sherbet, 199
County Fair Chocolate Cake, 191
Creamy Orange Pops, 197
Crème de Menthe Sheet Cake, 94
Deluxe Ice Cream Sandwiches, 201
Easy Strawberry Ice Cream, 196
End Zone Brownies, 18
Favorite Peanut Butter Cookies, 9
French Chocolate Balls, 95
Fresh Fruit Ices, 203
Fresh Peach Ice Cream, 194
Fresh Peach Pie, 187
Frosty Chocolate-Pecan Pie, 90
Fruit Meringue Chantilly, 112
Fudge-Topped Cherry Hearts, 137
Ghostly Parfaits, 22
Honeydew Sorbet, 199
Hot Fudge Sauce, 98
Hot Fudge Topping, 204
Iced Shamrock Cookies, 113
Ladyfingers, 136
Lone Star Pecan Cake, 215
Maple Indian Pudding, 50
Mother's Luscious Chocolate Cake, 147
Orange-Filled Napoleons, 195
Peanut Butter Round-Up Cookies, 214
Prize-Winning Apple Pie, 189
Raspberry Crumble, 111
Raspberry Pops, 197
Rich Rum Cake, 86
Spicy Pumpkin Pie, 51
Springtime Cake Roll, 125
Strawberry Shortcake, 170

Sweet Chocolate Chunk Cookies, 91
Violet Layer Cake, 158
Walnut Torte, 68
White Chocolate Chip-Macadamia Nut Brownie Pie, 93
White Chocolate Mousse Pastries, 96
Wild Blueberry Ice, 198

Mains

Baked Country Ham, 120
Broiled Chicken Breasts with Lime, 211
Filet Mignons Flambé, 101
Grilled Garlic Burgers, 164
Grilled Steaks with Herb-Mustard Sauce, 175
Herb-Roasted Chicken with Spring Vegetables, 121
Honey Spiced Ham, 74
Lime & Ginger Grilled Salmon, 165
Midnight Moon Sandwiches, 20
New England Boiled Dinner, 106
Overnight Pork & Sauerkraut, 83
Pan-Fried Trout, 176
Picnic Barbecued Chicken Sandwiches, 8
Prime Rib Roast with Yorkshire Pudding, 63
Roast Cornish Hens, 100
Sage-Roasted Turkey, 42
Salami Submarine with Olive Salad, 15
Smothered Hot Dogs, 16
Stuffed Roast Duck, 45
Texas Border Barbecued Beef Ribs, 210

Miscellaneous

Apple Relish, 187
Blueberry Syrup, 204
Cranberry-Orange Chutney, 75
Fresh Corn-Tomato Salsa, 213
Herb Butter Blend, 114
Papaya Salsa, 213

Index

Peach Butter, 192
Peachy Cinnamon Jam, 186
Quick Bread & Butter Pickles, 190
Strawberry Preserves, 205

Salads
Blue Cheese Potato Salad, 164
Confetti Salad, 16
Cucumber-Yogurt Salad, 119
Curried Chicken Salad, 131
Frozen Christmas Salad, 66
Ginger-Lime Salad, 170
Greek Salad in a Pita Pocket, 156
Minted Pea Salad, 155
Strawberry-Spinach Salad, 146
Summer Vegetable Salad, 168
Tempting Caesar Salad, 99
World's Greatest Pie Crust, 188

Sides
Asparagus with Tomato Vinaigrette, 122
Baked Artichokes with
   Mustard-Butter Sauce, 62
Broccoli with Orange Sauce, 49
Buttery Roasted Potatoes, 177
Colcannon, 107
Cornbread Stuffing with Sage
   & Sausage, 43
Creamed Onions with Peanuts, 64
Creamed Peas, 166
Fresh Corn Cakes, 178
Fresh Cranberry Ring, 48
Glazed Carrots, 65
Grilled Vegetable Skewers, 167
Herbed Mashed Potatoes, 46
Mummy's Corn Pudding, 21
Pears with Cranberry Relish, 65
Rice Pilaf with Carrots, 123

Roasted Baby Red Potatoes, 102
Roasted Corn with Rosemary
   Butter, 169
Sautéed Tomatoes with Tarragon, 142
Scalloped Oysters, 44
Scalloped Sweet Potatoes, 47
Sesame Asparagus, 154
Sour Cream Mashed Potatoes, 64
Spicy Grilled Vegetables, 212
Spinach-Onion Casserole, 110
Stuffed Zucchini, 185

Soups & Stews
Basic Chicken Broth, 34
Burgundy Beef Stew, 30
Buttery Squash Soup, 98
Chicken Soup with Wild Rice
   & Mushrooms, 34
Chunky Gazpacho, 174
Cream of Broccoli Soup, 32
Creamy Crab Bisque, 57
French Onion Soup with Toasted
   Rye & Gruyere, 26
Halftime Tomato-Basil Soup, 14
Hoppin' John, 81
Italian Wedding Soup, 31
Mediterranean Peasant Soup, 28
New England Clam Chowder, 35
Potato Rivel Soup, 85
Potato Soup, 108
Potato-Cheddar Chowder, 29
Split Pea Soup with Ham, 33
Spring Pea Soup, 118
Tortilla Soup, 209
Vegetable Stew, 27

We've cooked up a whole collection of Gooseberry Patch® books!

Have a taste for more? Call us toll-free at

1-800-854-6673

We'll send you our latest catalog filled with kitchenware, candles, handmade quilts, gourmet goodies, enamelware, bowls, bubble night lights and our very own line of cookbooks, calendars and organizers!

Phone us:
1·800·854·6673

Fax us:
1·740·363·7225

Visit our website.
www.gooseberrypatch.com

Send us your favorite recipe!

*and the memory that makes it special for you!** If we select your recipe for a brand new **Gooseberry Patch** cookbook, your name will appear right along with it...and you'll receive a FREE copy of the book! Mail to:

Vickie & Jo Ann
Gooseberry Patch, Dept. Book
600 London Road
Delaware, Ohio 43015

*Please include the number of servings and all other necessary information!

spring fever ♥ apple blossoms ❀ tulips & daffodils Easter baskets ★

farmers' market ★ June brides ★ strawberry shortcake ★ lemonade stands ★ front porch swing ★

freshly cut pine ✳ Christmas carols ✳ cocoa by the fire ✳ family & friends ✳ paper snowflakes ✳ Christmas carols

first day of school ☙ autumn leaves ☙ jack-'o-lanterns ☙ turkey dressing